Hymns and Fragments

The Lockert Library of Poetry in Translation

EDITORIAL ADVISOR: Daryl Hine

For other titles in the Lockert Library see page 287

Friedrich Hölderlin

Hymns and Fragments

TRANSLATED AND INTRODUCED

BY Richard Sieburth

Princeton University Press   Princeton, New Jersey

Published by Princeton University Press, 41 William Street,
Princeton, New Jersey 08540
In the United Kingdom: Princeton University Press
Chichester, West Sussex

Library of Congress Cataloging in Publication Data
Hölderlin, Friedrich, 1770-1843.
Hymns and fragments.

(The Lockert library of poetry in translation)
Bibliography: p.
Includes indexes.
I. Sieburth, Richard. II. Title. III. Series.
PT2359.H2A6 1984   831′.6   84-3390
ISBN 0-691-06607-8 (alk. paper)
ISBN 0-691-01412-4 (pbk.)

The Lockert Library of Poetry in Translation is supported
by a bequest from Charles Lacy Lockert (1888-1974)

This book has been composed in Linotron Galliard type

Princeton University Press books are printed on acid-free paper
and meet the guidelines for permanence and durability of the
Committee on Production Guidelines for Book Longevity of the
Council on Library Resources

Printed in the United States of America

10 9 8 7

http://pup.princeton.edu

For Anna

Wem sonst als dir

Contents

Acknowledgments

ANYONE who has approached Hölderlin owes deep gratitude to the work of Adolf Beck, Friedrich Beissner, M. B. Benn, Pierre Bertaux, Wolfgang Binder, Bernhard Böschenstein, André du Bouchet, François Fédier, Emery George, Cyrus Hamlin, R. B. Harrison, Philippe Jaccottet, Walther Killy, Philippe Lacoue-Labarthe, Paul de Man, Christopher Middleton, Günter Mieth, Rainer Nägele, Gustave Roud, Lawrence Ryan, D. E. Sattler, Wolfgang Schadewaldt, Jochen Schmidt, George Steiner, Peter Szondi, Richard Unger, and Rolf Zuberbühler. I would like to acknowledge a particular debt to Michael Hamburger, who, over the course of the past thirty years, has been almost singlehandedly responsible for making Hölderlin available to English-speaking readers. James Clifford, Benedict Fitzgerald, Peter Laurie, and Siegfried de Rachewiltz have been crucial friends to this project from the very outset; it has also benefited from the encouragements of D. S. Carne-Ross, Robert Fitzgerald, Francis Golffing, and Richard Howard. I would also like to thank the editors of *Canto, Agenda, St. Andrews Review, The Harvard Advocate,* and *OARS* in which some of these translations first appeared. Grateful acknowledgment is made to Verlag W. Kohlhammer, publishers of the *Grosse Stuttgarter Ausgabe,* and to Verlag Roter Stern, publishers of the *Frankfurter Ausgabe,* for their kind permission to reprint the German texts of Hölderlin's poems.

Translator's Note

THIS SELECTION of hymns and fragments contains the near totality of Hölderlin's work in free rhythms between 1801 and 1806. Though it properly belongs among his hymns, I have excluded the somewhat earlier "Wie Wenn am Feiertage" (1799–1800). The only other major works omitted for reasons of space are "Germanien" and "Friedensfeier" (both composed in early 1801). I have included one poem at the end of the volume that is considerably later than the rest; some scholars doubt its authenticity altogether. One way of reading this book is to start there and page backward.

Chronology

1770   March 20. Johann Christian Friedrich Hölderlin born in Lauffen on the Neckar (Swabia).

1772   Death of his father; birth of a sister, Heinrike.

1774   Remarriage of his mother to Johann Christoph Gok, burgomaster of Nürtingen.

1776   Birth of his half-brother, Karl Gok.

1779   Death of his stepfather.

1780   Begins piano lessons; later studies the flute.

1784   Enters the Lower Monastery School at Denkendorf, near Nürtingen. Chafes at the rigidly disciplinary atmosphere. Discovers the poetry of Schiller and Klopstock and writes his first verses.

1786   Enters the Higher Monastery School at Maulbronn. Falls in love with Louise Nast and becomes close friends with her cousin, Immanuel. Continues to read Schiller and Klopstock, as well as Young and Ossian. Begins to doubt his religious vocation.

1788   Enters the Lutheran theological seminary (Stift) in Tübingen. Founds a poetry association with his friends Neuffer and Magenau and makes the acquaintance of fellow seminarian Hegel.

1789   Breaks off his engagement to Louise Nast. Writes his first poems inspired by the French Revolution. Duke Karl Eugen places student activities at the Stift under close surveillance.

1790   Obtains his degree of *Magister*. Increasingly close emotional and intellectual bonds with fellow students Schelling and Hegel. Reads Kant and Rousseau, as well as Leibniz, Spinoza, and Plato. Falls in love with Elise Lebret.

1791   Travels to Switzerland to visit the site of the Rütli oath; meets Lavater in Zürich. Publishes his first poems in the *Musenalmanach* of the political journalist Stäudlin. Headaches and depressions.

1792   War between France and the Austro-Prussian coalition. Sympathizes with France as the "defender of human rights" against "the abuse of princely power." Begins work on the novel *Hyperion*.

1793   Introduced to Schiller through Stäudlin. Hegel leaves the Stift for a post in Bern: they part on the words *Reich Gottes* ("May God's Kingdom Come"). Passes his final examinations in theology at the end of the year but is now certain that, against the wishes of his mother, he will never enter the ministry.

1794   On the recommendation of Schiller Hölderlin is employed by Charlotte von Kalb as tutor to her son in Waltershausen. Continues work on *Hyperion* and reads Kant and Fichte intensively, though he fears he may be losing himself in "the realm of abstraction." In November travels to Jena with his pupil, where he attends Fichte's lectures, meets Herder and Goethe, and is the frequent guest of Schiller, who publishes a fragment of *Hyperion* in his *Neuer Thalia*.

1795   Alarmed by his erratic discipline of her son, Charlotte von Kalb relieves Hölderlin from his post, while providing him with enough money to stay on several more months in Jena. Invited to collaborate on Schiller's magazine *Die Horen*. Corresponds with Hegel on Fichtean philosophy. On Schiller's recommendation Cotta agrees to publish *Hyperion*. Meetings with Fichte and Novalis. Friendship with Isaak von Sinclair, who is expelled from the university in the spring for participation in student disturbances. Hölderlin abruptly leaves Jena in June; returns home to Nürtingen in a deep depression, mired in "malady and discontent." Writes Schiller that fall: "I am frozen and numbed by the winter that surrounds me. My sky is as iron and I am as stone." Friends find him "dead to all sympathy ... a living corpse." Philosophical discussions with Schelling in Tübingen and Nürtingen, which eventually result in the so-called *Älteste Systemprogramm des deutschen Idealismus*, generally believed to have been the collaborative effort of Schelling, Hegel, and Hölderlin.

1796   Obtains a post as tutor in the household of the wealthy Frankfurt banker Gontard. Soon falls in love with Gontard's young wife, Susette, whom he hereafter refers to as "Diotima." In the wake of the French invasion of the Rhine valley Hölderlin in July accompanies Susette and her children to safety in Kassel, where they meet up with Wilhelm Heinse, author of *Ardinghello*, and proceed onward to Bad Driburg before returning to Frankfurt in September. Hegel dedicates a long oracular poem entitled "Eleusis" to Hölderlin.

1797   Despite the recent *coup d'état* in France Hölderlin remains convinced that the youth of Germany will soon bring about a "revolution in attitudes and conceptions which will make everything that has gone before turn red with shame." The first volume of *Hyperion* appears in April. He sends a copy to Schiller, along with two recent poems that the latter in turn passes on to Goethe, who judges them too "subjective," too "overstrained." In August Goethe receives Hölderlin in Frankfurt and finds him "somewhat depressed and sickly" yet "most amiable and . . . timidly open." Goethe advises him "to write short poems and to select for each of them an object of human interest." Begins work on a tragedy, *Empedokles*, in late summer.

1798   Political agitation in southern Germany for the establishment of an Alemannic Republic. Hölderlin increasingly disillusioned with Frankfurt milieu. Headaches and depressions. Tensions in Gontard household erupt into a crisis in late September: Hölderlin quits his post but will continue to meet and correspond secretly with Diotima over the next two years. In November he travels to the Rastatt Congress with Sinclair, now a jurist in the service of the Landgrave of Hessen–Homburg, and frequents radical political circles.

1799   Residence in Homburg. Close ties with Sinclair and the young republican poet Böhlendorff. Occasional visits to nearby Frankfurt for trysts with Diotima. Works on *Empedokles*, studies Pindar, writes a number of important theoretical essays dealing with philosophical and aesthetic issues. Hopes to secure his livelihood by founding a humanistic journal, *Iduna*, devoted to poetry and criticism. Writes Schiller, Goethe, and Schelling, among others, to solicit contributions but meets with little response: the project falls through. The second volume of *Hyperion* published in October: contains a scathing attack on contemporary Germany. Bonaparte named First Consul in November; Hölderlin considers him little more than "a species of dictator."

1800   Secretly meets with Diotima for the last time in May. Moves to Stuttgart in late June, where he resides with his friend Landauer and gives private lessons to support himself. Translates Pindar and writes a number of major elegies, among them "Brot und Wein."

1801   Arrives in Hauptwil (Switzerland) in mid-January to take up a private tutorship in the household of the family Gonzenbach. The Treaty of Lunéville is signed in February: prospects of peace inspire the hymn "Friedensfeier." Quits his post in mid-April and returns home to Nürtingen. Writes Schiller in June to inquire about the possibility of lecturing on Greek at Jena: no reply. Cotta agrees to publish a volume of selected poems the following spring: the book never sees print. Decides to accept a post in Bordeaux as tutor in the household of Daniel Meyer, wine merchant and consul of Hamburg. Sets off from Nürtingen in early December; writes Böhlendorff he is leaving Germany because "they have no use for me."

1802   Arrives in Bordeaux at the end of January and leaves abruptly after three months. Travels back to Germany in May and reaches Stuttgart in mid-June, "pale as a corpse, emaciated, with hollow wild eyes, long hair and beard, and dressed like a beggar." In early July receives word from Sinclair in Stuttgart that Diotima has died. Returns to Nürtingen and is placed in the care of a local physician. Has recovered sufficiently by early fall to travel to Regensburg with Sinclair. Meets the Landgrave of Homburg to whom "Patmos" will be dedicated the following January. Settles back in Nürtingen in the late fall: intensive work on "Patmos" and other hymns.

1803   Continues work on hymns and sends translations of Sophocles off to publishers. Visits Schelling in June. The latter, aghast at his friend's physical and mental condition, writes Hegel to ask whether he might be able to take care of Hölderlin in Jena. The reply is noncommittal. Sinclair, convinced that Hölderlin is still basically sound of mind, invites him to take up residence in Homburg again. The project is vetoed by Hölderlin's mother. Toward the end of the year he revises a number of *Nightsongs*.

1804   The translations of *Oedipus* and *Antigone* appear in two volumes in April. Sinclair arranges for Hölderlin to become court librarian to the Landgrave of Homburg. On their way to Homburg Hölderlin and Sinclair participate in a number of political discussions with Stuttgart radicals. Loose talk about assassinating the Elector of Württemberg will have severe repercussions the following year. Hölderlin takes up residence in Homburg in July.

1805   After a falling-out with Sinclair, a certain Blankenstein reports the subversive political discussions of the previous June to the authorities. Sinclair is arrested in February and placed under indictment for high treason. In the course of the investigation Hölderlin is implicated in the conspiracy but is adjudged mentally incompetent to stand trial. After four months under detention Sinclair is released in July for lack of evidence. Hölderlin spends the summer in a state of agitation.

1806   In July the state of Homburg is absorbed into the newly established Grand Duchy of Hessen–Darmstadt. Sinclair informs Hölderlin's mother that these political circumstances make it impossible for the landgrave to keep her son on in his employ; Hölderlin's condition, moreover, has reached the point where Sinclair fears for his friend's safety. In September he is transported by force to a psychiatric clinic in Tübingen and placed under "strict observation."

1807   After some ten months of unsuccessful treatment in the Autenrieth Clinic Hölderlin is released into the care of a local Tübingen carpenter and admirer of *Hyperion*, Ernst Zimmer. Doctors give him "at most three years" to live.

1822   Second edition of *Hyperion*.

1826   Publication of Hölderlin's *Selected Poems*, edited by Uhland and Schwab.

1843   7 June. Death of Hölderlin.

Hymns and Fragments

Introduction

Ihn zehret die Heimath.
Kolonien liebt, und tapfer Vergessen der Geist.   ("Brot und Wein")

IN EARLY December 1801 Hölderlin sets off on foot from his mother's house in the small Swabian town of Nürtingen; he is bound for Bordeaux, some thousand kilometers to the southwest, where a position awaits him as private tutor and minister in the household of a certain Herr Meyer, prosperous German wine merchant and consul of the city of Hamburg to the French port. "My decision to leave my native land, perhaps forever, has cost me bitter tears," he writes to his friend Böhlendorff on the eve of departure, "for there is nothing dearer to me in the world. But they have no use for me. Still, I shall and must remain German even if my needy heart and stomach drive me all the way to Tahiti."

Hölderlin is thirty-one years old. He has published an epistolary novel, *Hyperion*, and some sixty poems in various literary magazines; he has composed a verse tragedy, *Empedokles*, and is at work on translations of Pindar and on a series of ambitious hymns—or *vaterländische Gesänge*, as he calls them—celebrating the heroic destiny that awaits Germany upon the radiant return of the gods. He is also consumed by a deep sense of failure and isolation. His love affair with Susette Gontard (or "Diotima") has come to an unquiet end; his plans to found a literary journal with the aid of his friends Schelling and Schiller have fallen through, as have all hopes for the publication of a volume of his own verse. Above all, he finds himself without profession or intellectual station. Having refused to enter the Lutheran ministry for which he had been trained at the Tübingen seminary, he has had to live off the generosity of friends and periodic employ as private tutor in the houses of the wealthy bourgeoisie. His most recent attempt to secure a university post—a letter of inquiry to his erstwhile mentor, Schiller, about the possibility of lecturing on Greek at Jena—has met with no reply. There is simply no room for him in Germany. By mid-December he has crossed into France.

Of the events of the next six months very little is known. Hölderlin's self-imposed exile to France constitutes a kind of caesura in his career, an enigmatic gap that surviving letters and documents only partially serve to fill. Detained for two weeks by local authorities in Strasbourg while his travel visa clears with Paris, he proceeds on to Lyons, where, thanks to a conscientious bureaucrat, an official portrait of the poet is preserved in the police register:

> AGE: *32 years*, HEIGHT: *one meter, 766 millimeters*, HAIR AND EYEBROWS: *chestnut brown*, EYES: *brown*, NOSE: *medium*, MOUTH: *small*, CHIN: *round*, FOREHEAD: *covered*, FACE: *oval*.

On January 28 Hölderlin is in Bordeaux, apparently having covered most of the intervening six hundred kilometers on foot. Upon arrival he writes a letter home to his family that hints at a harrowing *nox animae* experienced somewhere in the mountains of the Auvergne, alone, in the dead of winter, fearing for his life and mind. "I have gone through so much that I can barely speak of it now. For the past few days I have been wandering through a beautiful springtime [i.e., down the valleys of the Périgord], but just prior to this, on the fearsome snow-covered heights of the Auvergne, in the midst of storms and wilderness, during ice-cold nights with my loaded pistol by my side in my rough bed— it was then that I said the finest prayer of my life, a prayer I shall never forget. I am safe—give thanks with me." The letter closes, somewhat oracularly, with assurances to his mother that he has come through his baptism of ice "born anew," ready to face the world with fresh resolve, "tempered through and through and initiated [or ordained] as is your wish."

In Bordeaux Hölderlin takes up residence in the severe elegance of Consul Meyer's neoclassical townhouse; his duties involve the education of six children, of whom he speaks affectionately in rare letters home. Over the course of the early spring he accompanies the family to its country estate in the Médoc. The landscape will inscribe itself deeply into his memory:

> But go now and greet
> The lovely Garonne
> And the gardens of Bordeaux,
> There, where the path cuts
> Along the shore and the stream dives
> Riverward . . .   ("Remembrance")

He also ventures along the coast toward Les Landes, or so it would seem from a letter written to Böhlendorff the following fall: "I saw the sad, solitary earth and the shepherds of southern France and individual beauties, men and women, who have grown up in the fear of political uncertainty and of hunger. The mighty element, the fire of heaven, and the silence of the inhabitants, their life amid nature, their narrow existence and contentment, moved me no end, and as one says of heroes, I can well say I was struck by Apollo."

"Struck by Apollo." How literally is one to take this? In Hölderlin's idiom the image usually refers to the devastating visitation of divine fire upon mortals, or to the sudden blinding light of madness by which the gods signal their perilous immediacy to heroes and seers. It is an experience to which his later hymns and fragments will frequently allude, often associated with the hammering sun of southern France. The urgency of the landscape can barely be contained by syntax:

> Thus like starlings
> With screams of joy, when above Gascogne, regions
>   of countless gardens,
> When fountains, where olives grow
> On lovely foreign soil, when trees
> By grassy paths,
> Unaware in the wild,
> Are stung by the sun
> And earth's heart
> Opens . . .   ("The Nearest the Best")

In mid-May, for reasons that remain obscure, Hölderlin abruptly decides, like the starlings evoked above, to make his migration homeward. Quitting his comfortable post in the Meyer household, he heads north by mail coach (perhaps passing through Paris), and by June 7 is back at the German border at Strasbourg, his wanderings of the past six months now come full circle.

At some point toward the end of the month he appears at the house of the writer Matthison in Stuttgart, "pale as a corpse, emaciated, with hollow wild eyes, long hair and beard, and dressed like a beggar." Shortly thereafter he returns home to Nürtingen, displaying (according to his half-brother) "the clearest indications of mental derangement." In early July he is in Stuttgart again, where he receives word that Diotima—Susette Gontard—has died. The shock is apparently too much: back home in Nürtingen, he is placed by his family in the care of a local physician whose son reads the poet passages from Homer to calm his periodic "outbreaks of fury." He passes the summer in a state of agitation but has sufficiently recovered by fall to undertake the composition of "Patmos," his most ambitious poem to date, especially commissioned by the Landgrave of Homburg. He sets to work, moreover, on a number of new hymns, prepares his translations of Sophocles' *Oedipus* and *Antigone* for publication, and continues to haruspicate Pindar's odes. Over the course of the next four years, under the ever-mounting pressure of vision, Hölderlin will produce the hymns and fragments upon which his reputation as the first great modern of European poetry rests. In late 1806, at age thirty-six, he is committed to a Tübingen clinic for the insane.

> *But the beauty is not the madness*
> *Tho' my errors and wrecks lie about me.* (Ezra Pound, "Canto CXVI")

To imply that Hölderlin's late hymns and fragments are the products of his incipient insanity, or that his madness was somehow precipitated by his ill-fated voyage to France of 1802, is of course to oversimplify and to considerably falsify the question. As Michel Foucault has pointed out in his essay "Hölderlin et le 'non' du père,"[1] it is specious to assume that these texts can be explained away as the effects of a discrete series of biographical causes; if anything, they serve to illuminate the very *discontinu*-ities that define the problematic relation of life to work, madness to poetry, events to words. The mystique of madness has none-theless attended Hölderlin's reputation from the early nineteenth century down to our day. Friedrich Schlegel and Bettina von Arnim romanticized it as the particular sign of his prophetic elec-tion, and a century later the German expressionists read it as a tragic prefiguration of the destiny of Nietzsche and their own poetic generation. In France surrealism did much to contribute to the nimbus of derangement surrounding Hölderlin's name. The first translations of his late work were published by Jouve and Klossowski, significantly enough, under the title *Poèmes de la folie d'Hölderlin* (1930), and these versions in turn inspired David Gascoyne's surrealist *Hölderlin's Madness* (1938).

But what does it mean to speak of Hölderlin's madness? Is it something that can be confidently assigned an etiology or a name? The official record (such as it is) tells us he lost his mind toward the end of 1806. Hospitalized in a clinic recently founded by a disciple of Benjamin Franklin's theories of the moral rehabilita-tion of the insane, he is released after a year's unsuccessful treat-ment into the care of a local cabinetmaker and admirer, Ernst Zimmer. Hölderlin lives out the remainder of his days in a small tower overlooking the river Neckar—lost, according to most contemporaries, in some nocturnal region of madness (or *Um-nachtung*) where for the next thirty-six years he will pass his time playing the piano and flute, reading the classics, going for long walks, receiving, with exaggerated deference, occasional visitors, and, under the mysterious heteronym of Scardanelli, now and

[1] An English version is included in *Language, Counter-Memory, Practice: Se-lected Essays and Interviews by Michel Foucault* (Ithaca, 1977). My discussion of the question of Hölderlin's madness also draws on perspectives suggested by Pierre Bertaux's *Friedrich Hölderlin* (Frankfurt am Main, 1978).

then composing a few small rhymed poems more notable for their melancholy sweetness than for their visionary fire.

Biographers have variously dated the origins of the night that descended over the entire second half of Hölderlin's life. Some locate its beginnings in the spring of 1802 beneath the blazing sun of southern France or in the catastrophic news of Diotima's death later that summer. Others turn the calendar further back and focus on the acute depression that led Hölderlin to flee Jena in mid-1795, numbed by a crisis whose features curiously anticipate his subsequent breakdowns. In the end, however, chronology can tell us very little: as Foucault suggests, the truth of madness lies outside of history and, to that extent, remains forever mute.

Repeated attempts have nonetheless been made to make Hölderlin's madness *speak*—or, more precisely, to label and locate it within a precise taxonomy of mental disease. Most of the recent medical literature on Hölderlin has diagnosed his condition as a form of cyclothymic schizophrenia, characterized by manic depressive oscillations in mood; earlier studies in turn classed him as a victim of *dementia praecox catatonica*.[2] The medical documents of Hölderlin's own day are, by contrast, considerably vaguer

[2] Jean Laplanche's 1961 *Hölderlin et la question du père* is a marked exception to the general level of psychiatric commentary on Hölderlin. Analyzing the poet's precarious emotional equilibrium from 1794 to 1800, Laplanche interprets Hölderlin's radical swings in mood as arising from the essential instability of his configuration of "object relations" and, more specifically, from his problematic rapport with the authority represented by the figure of the Father (Laplanche focuses especially on Hölderlin's ambivalent adulation of Schiller and Fichte). Hölderlin lost his own father at two and his stepfather at nine, and the vacancy left by these deaths, Laplanche argues, was a gaping space Hölderlin would forever refuse to fill. This *forclusion* (in Lacan's terminology) of the Law of the Father—who, symbolically or no, limits the unbounded relationship of mother and child and hence institutes that principle of diacritical difference on which all systems of signification are necessarily founded—in turn would explain why Hölderlin's discourse is continually drawn toward some fundamental absence, why silence progressively wells up at the center of his song. Laplanche's approach at least has the virtue of employing an analytical framework supple enough to describe the intricate relation between schizophrenia and poetry in terms of a linguistic disorder grounded in a crisis of the signifier.

as to the precise nature of his affliction: some speak of hypochondria, others refer to melancholy or periodic mania, but the majority have recourse to such designations as *trauriger Zustand* ("sad condition"), *Zerrüttung* ("confusion" or "derangement"), or, toward the end, *Umnachtung* ("benightedness").

Nor is the testimony of Hölderlin's own family and acquaintances any more conclusive. Take Schelling's description to Hegel of their mutual friend's state in the summer of 1803, a year after his return from Bordeaux:

> Since his fatal trip, his mind has become entirely unhinged, and although he is still able to do work—for example, to translate Greek up to a certain point—he has nevertheless completely lost his wits. I was shocked by his aspect: he neglects his appearance in the most disgusting fashion and, although his conversation shows fewer signs of derangement, he has taken on the outward mannerisms of those in this condition. There is little hope for his recovery here.

A curious feature of this portrait is the insinuation that Hölderlin may have somehow deliberately cultivated the demeanor of madness. Isaak von Sinclair, the person closest to Hölderlin during this period, makes this very point in a letter to the poet's mother the following year: "What appears to be his disturbance of mind [*Gemüths Verwirrung*] is in fact a mode of expression he has adopted on well-considered grounds."

Indeed, there may have been compelling legal reasons for Hölderlin to play at Hamlet. In the summer of 1804, while traveling to Homburg to take up a position as court librarian to Landgrave Friedrich, Hölderlin had spent some time in Stuttgart frequenting his friend Sinclair's circle of political activists and adventurers. In the course of discussions there had apparently been a certain amount of loose talk about assassinating the archconservative Elector of Württemberg and establishing a revolutionary Swabian Republic—Sinclair had been a student radical at Jena, and Hölderlin never abandoned his early Jacobin sympathies. One of the group, however, subsequently took it upon himself to denounce the lot to the local authorities, and, as a result, Sinclair was arrested the following February on charges of high treason and held for four months before being released for lack of evidence. When Hölderlin learned that he had also been implicated in the alleged assassination plot, his condition apparently took a turn for the worse: contemporary accounts report him ranting over and over, "I refuse to be a Jacobin, down with all Jacobins!" This agitated behavior convinced his protector, the Landgrave of Homburg, to intervene in the legal proceedings to certify Hölderlin's mental incompetence to stand trial. A doctor's testimony to the commission further corroborated his unsoundness of mind. According to the deposition, the poet had lapsed into a state of complete incoherence (speaking an idiom described as "half German, half Greek, half Latin"), and his folly, moreover, had degenerated into severe frenzy. The case against Hölderlin was dismissed.

Though he may have merely played the fool as a legal ploy, Hölderlin emerged from his brush with the law profoundly scathed. William Blake, brought to trial on trumped-up charges of sedition, had undergone a similar ordeal the previous year— and, in a sense, the fate of both poets is emblematic of the plight of radical political and/or imaginative vision during the era of reaction following the French Revolution. Whereas Blake managed to find retreat in the privacy of his later prophecies, Hölderlin never seemed to regain his equilibrium after the events of 1805. The last glimpse we get of him before his commitment is an eyewitness account dated September 11, 1806:

> This morning they took poor Hölterling [sic] away to his relatives [i.e., to the Autenrieth Clinic in Tübingen]. He did everything he could to throw himself out of the vehicle, but the attendant in charge pushed him back in again. Screaming that he was being abducted by military guards [Hatschiere], and redoubling his efforts to escape, Hölterling scratched the attendant with his enormously long fingernails until the man was completely bloodied.

A vignette that might have been culled from the pages of Foucault's *Madness and Civilization*: Hölderlin emerges as a violent figure of the Other, banished from the enlightened precincts of Reason and relegated to the silent, carceral space reserved for the criminal, the visionary, or the insane.

> *So komm! daß wir das Offene suchen,*
> *Daß ein Eigenes wir suchen, so weit es auch ist.*   ("Brot und Wein")

Hölderlin's entire oeuvre pursues a precarious dialogue with the Other—whether this take the form of madness, revolution, or those gods of ancient Greece whose vanished immediacies are celebrated in his early elegies and odes. His journey to Bordeaux is perhaps the most literal instance of this dialectic, for by leaving Germany, by turning away from native ground, he was deliberately venturing into an alien space, prepared, as he wrote Böhlendorff on the eve of departure, to lay himself open to the lightning (his chosen "sign," he explained, for the manifestation of the divine). His only fear was that he might "end up like Tantalus who had more of the gods than he could digest." Surfeit of ecstasy, transgression, punishment from on high—this may be in part what Hölderlin was alluding to when he later spoke of having been "struck by Apollo" in southern France, dazed by an intensity he could scarcely contain:

> Since men sense more
> In the scorch
> Of deserts,
> Drunk with light, and the spirit of animals
> Rests with them. But soon, like a dog in hot weather,
> My voice shall amble through alleys of gardens
> In which people live
> In France   ("We set out from the abyss . . .")

Wandering through the blaze of the Midi, Hölderlin discovered he had intruded into the perilous realm of the Other: the very ground burned with the fire of archaic Greece.

"The athletic character of the southern peoples, among the ruins of the spirit of antiquity," he would later recollect, "made me more familiar with the true essence of the Greeks; I came to understand their nature and their wisdom, the way their bodies grew in their climate and the restraint they adopted to protect their exuberant genius from the violence of the element." The traces of Apollo's violent fire were everywhere: in the "savage, warlike and purely virile quality" of the local populace, in the "light of life" that leapt in their limbs and eyes, in the "virtuosity" with which (like the tragic heroes of Hellas) they "experienced the sensation of death, satisfying their thirst for knowledge," and, above all, in the sheer rush of Mediterranean sensation:

> where nostrils
> Nearly ache with the rising
> Scent of lemon and oil from Provence, such gratitude
> Have the lands of Gascogne
> Granted me.　　("We set out from the abyss . . .")

Visiting a collection of ancient statuary (presumably in the new Musée Napoléon in Paris), Hölderlin discovered the same fusion of clarity and conflagration, of vulnerability and vigor, that he had observed in the landscape and inhabitants of southern France. He was struck above all by the "tenderness" (*Zärtlichkeit*) of the Greek body, by the delicacy of its stamina; and in the silent, ingathered poise of classical sculpture—intense movement coinciding with repose, fire informing each definition of detail—he discerned the essential feature of all great art. Such certainty of purpose, such self-assurance, he noted, was the supreme kind of representation, "the highest form of the sign."

Though his journey to France had therefore brought Hölderlin as close as he had ever come to experiencing Hellas firsthand, it nevertheless confirmed his profoundly dialectical vision of the relation between modern and ancient, northern and southern, German and Greek. His fullest statement concerning these contraries is contained, significantly enough, in the letter he wrote Böhlendorff on December 4, 1801, just before setting off for

Bordeaux. It is worth quoting at some length, since it sheds light on the tensions that inform his later hymns and fragments. Hölderlin's argument is grounded in a series of antitheses that juxtapose the distinctive traits of modern Western (or "Hesperidean") poetry (to which "Junonian sobriety" and "clarity of representation" are intrinsic) with the poetry of the ancient Greeks (whose native impulse instead lies in "holy pathos" and the Apollonian "fire from heaven"):

> Nothing is more difficult for us to learn than to make free use of our national traits. And I believe that clarity of representation is originally as natural to us as the fire of heaven is to the Greeks. This is precisely why it should be easier to surpass them in beautiful passion . . . than in their Homeric presence of mind and gift for representation.
>
> This sounds like a paradox. But I repeat, and leave it up to you to judge and make use of it as you wish: In the course of the progress of culture, the specifically national element will always prove to be the lesser advantage. This is why the Greeks have little mastery over holy pathos, since this was innate to them; by contrast, from Homer onwards they excel in their gift for representation because this extraordinary man had enough spirit to plunder the *Junonian sobriety* of the Occident for the benefit of his own Apollonian kingdom, thus truly appropriating the foreign element as his own.
>
> With us, the opposite holds true. . . .

In other words, while the Greek poet quests after, and achieves, clarity or sobriety (which is *not* something native to his passionate national temper), the Hesperidean or German poet in turn strives for "holy pathos" in order to counterbalance his own innate rationality.

The particular paradox that Hölderlin underscores, however, points to the fact that it is far easier to succeed at something foreign or extrinsic (say, as the Greeks excel in precision and restraint) than to realize one's own inborn capacities to the full. For a modern to imitate the ancients is therefore just as futile as to ignore the lesson of their otherness. It is only through the interchange of opposites—of desire and lucidity, of innate and acquired traits—that one can come to recognize what is truly one's own:

> But we must master what is native to us to the same extent as what is foreign. For this reason the Greeks are indispensable to us. But it is precisely in that which is native or national to us that we will never achieve their level, for, as mentioned, the most difficult thing is the *free* usage of what is *our own*.

The nearest, inmost things are the most arduous to seize (Tantalus again). It is only by venturing abroad, by passage into the Other, that we learn the way back. Hölderlin's schoolmate Hegel would argue something similar in his *Phenomenology*. The plot is as old as Homer.

The particular dialectical motion described in Hölderlin's letter to Böhlendorff weaves through many of his late hymns and fragments. It most frequently expresses itself as an interplay of heat and coolness, sun and shade. In his poem "The Ister," for example, borrowing Pindar's evocation of the journey of Hercules to the land of the Hyperboreans, Hölderlin imagines the Danube welcoming the demigod to Swabia:

> So it does not
> Surprise me he had
> Hercules as a guest,
> Far-shining, up from Olympos,
> Having left the Isthmos heat
> In search of shade,
> For though they had great fortitude
> In that place, spirits also need
> The cool.

According to legend, it was from the land of the Hyperboreans that Hercules brought back the olive trees he subsequently planted around the unshaded Olympic fields: just as the southern sun is mitigated by the imported shadow of the north, so (Hölderlin implies) Greece will return to itself through mediation of Germany.

The process, however, can also flow in the opposite direction. The genealogical myth of "The Migration" recounts the easterly journey of a "German tribe" down the Danube; upon reaching the Black Sea, the northern settlers intermarry with the meridional "children of the sun" in a *conjunctio oppositorum* that will give birth to the subsequent perfection of Hellas: "And from these sacred unions/A race arose, more beautiful than anything/By the name of man/Before or since." The same motion is repeated in "Patmos." At the outset of the poem the poet is seized by a spirit who whisks him away from "the shady woods and restless brooks of home" and bears him through the heavens into the dazzling rising sun of Asia. The voyage is at once spatial and temporal: the journey from west to east coincides with a progression from the darkness of the present to the radiance of the Hellenic and biblical past. At the conclusion of the poem the light of divine revelation (now filtered through the dark mediating lens of Holy Scripture) returns to Germany to provide illumination for the future:

> Yet many timid
> Eyes await a glimpse
> Of the light, reluctant
> To flower in the glare,
> Their courage bridled by the gold.
> But when the quiet radiant force of holy scripture falls
> As from the threshold of brows
> Oblivious to the world,
> They can exercise
> Their silent gaze,
> Rejoicing in grace.

In the poems inspired by Hölderlin's journey to Bordeaux another variation on this pattern emerges: the cool northeasterly breezes that blow from Germany beckon starlings back to sobriety from their seasonal exile in the Mediterranean sun:

> but when
> The breeze carves its way
> And the sharp northeasterly
> Quickens their eyes, they fly up,
> And at every corner
> Lovelier things draw into their sight,
> For they cleave to what is nearest . . .
>
> ("The Nearest the Best")

But what is nearest, Hölderlin's letter to Böhlendorff reminds us, is precisely what seems furthest from hand, which is why the path homeward lies through foreign lands. "Struck by Apollo" in the sear of southern France, having verged for a brief interval on perilous identity with the Other, Hölderlin swerves from the lightning, and, by a kind of dialectical reversal (or *vaterländische Umkehr*), turns back to native ground. His circuit resembles the flight of bees evoked in a late draft:

> When, drunk on the scent
> Of Spring, they are stirred
> By the spirit of the sun, driven
> Erratic in its pursuit, but when
> Burnt by a ray, they all veer back
> Abuzz, filled with premonition
>   above
>   the oak tree rustles   ("When the Sap . . .")

Icarus in miniature: the attraction of moth to star, the yearning of the soul to rejoin its source—punished, at the very apogee of delight, by the proximity of the fire.

> *Zwar leben die Götter*
> *Aber über dem Haupt droben in anderer Welt.*   ("Brot und Wein")

In the dense, Delphic commentaries that accompany his translations of *Oedipus* and *Antigone* (1804) Hölderlin compares the highest moment of tragic emotion (he uses the French term _transport_) to the role of caesura in prosody: both define a space in between, an "antirhythmic suspension" of temporal progression, an interval of silence in which the "pure Word" may appear. In this hiatus man and god couple and come asunder, taking distance on each other by the very paradox of their collision. The fragile exchange between mortals and gods, however, is forever threatened by man's restless reach beyond his rightful bounds. "No action, no thought can reach the extent of your desire," writes Hölderlin in an early draft of _Hyperion_, "This is the glory of man, that nothing ever suffices" (or, as Blakes phrases it, "the bounded is loathed by its possessor. . . . Less than All cannot satisfy Man"). Hölderlin's vision of man's ceaseless striving after the infinite is at once profoundly Greek and at the same time recognizably Romantic. Throughout his work the torrential course of rivers embodies (as it does in many of Goethe's Sturm und Drang lyrics) the exuberant impatience with all constraint. In "The Rhine," for example, the youthful river is an infant Hercules, victoriously fending off the snakes placed in his cradle by jealous Hera:

> His Word is hence a shout of joy.
> Unlike other children, he does not
> Whimper in swaddling clothes;
> For when riverbanks start
> Sidling up to him, crooked,
> Coiled in thirst,
> Eager to draw him, unawares,
> Into the shelter
> Of their teeth, he laughs
> And tears these snakes apart,
> Plunging onward with the spoils . . .

The young Rhine of this strophe belongs to a class of heroic overreachers that also includes Goethe's Faust, Blake's Orc, and Shelley's Prometheus. Hölderlin's confidence in human aspiration, however, is constantly balanced by an awareness of the dangers of Titanic excess. One of his late drafts beautifully evokes the destructive energies inherent in what he sometimes terms the "aorgic" drive of unbounded desire, here likened to the inchoate "sprouting of/rank envious/weeds," nature running riot:

> It grasps
> And spreads with too much fury. And like fire
> Consuming houses, lashes
> Out, uncaring, and spares
> No space and covers paths,
> Seething everywhere, a smothering cloud
> > wilderness without end.
> Seeking to pass for something
> Godly.   ("But when the gods . . .")

Confronted with such presumption, the heavenly powers are swift to react. Just as art (or culture) serves to check the chaotic forces of nature, so the gods are ever mindful to reimpose order on confusion, to re-establish boundaries where differentiation has been lost. They see to it that hubris is punished, for they ordain

> That he shall break his own
> Home, curse those he loves
> Like enemies, and bury father and child
> Under rubble, should he seek
> To become their equal, fanatic,
> Refusing to observe distinctions.   ("The Rhine")

The gods visit their punishment upon men in a variety of ways. One of their most enigmatic strategies is to overwhelm their favorites with the unexpected prodigality of divine presence:

> Which is why surprise and fright
> Strike mortal man
> When he considers the heaven
> He has heaped upon his shoulders
> With loving arms, and realizes
> The burden of joy;
> . . . .
> For misfortune is heavy
> To bear, and fortune weighs yet more.   ("The Rhine")

Behind this bewilderment with bliss lies a humility or *pietas* that is perhaps unique to Hölderlin among modern poets. What mortal, after all, could deserve the spendthrift generosity of the gods? What vessel (or what word) could contain the fullness they so recklessly squander on the earth? But the moods and motives of the divine are as unpredictable as its guise:

> Try taking it by surprise, and it turns
> To a dream; try matching it by force,
> And punishment is the reward.
> Often, when you've barely given it
> A thought, it just happens.   ("The Migration")

Such unwarranted moments of grace are more than most mortals can sustain. One of the most salient tropes of Hölderlin's mature work therefore involves the way in which man responds to the blinding day of the gods by reverting to the shelter of night:

> But someone reach me
> A fragrant cupful
> Of dark light, that
> I might rest; it would be sweet
> To drowse in the shade.   ("Remembrance")

The destiny of Rousseau in "The Rhine" further exemplifies this pattern of retreat: his exile on the island of St. Pierre ("In the shade of the woods,/Away from the burn of light,/Amid the fresh foliage of Lake Bienne") constitutes a deliberate flight from the drunken fire of divine inspiration.

But though their dialogue be fraught with peril, men and gods can occasionally achieve a perfect harmony, as the conclusion of "The Rhine" implies:

> Men and gods then celebrate their marriage,
> Every living thing rejoices,
> And for a while
> Fate achieves a balance.

This apocalyptic marriage of heaven and earth is of course a familiar feature of what has sometimes been defined as the "High

Romantic Argument."[3] Hölderlin, however, diverges from the "spousal verse" of a Wordsworth by his more dialectical (and more Hellenic) vision of the mutuality of men and gods:

> If there be
> One thing they need
> It is heroes and men
> And mortals in general. Since
> The gods feel nothing
> Of themselves, if to speak so
> Be permitted, they need
> Someone else to share and feel
> In their name . . .   ("The Rhine")

As Heidegger observes in his commentaries on Hölderlin, men and gods, at once distinct and interdependent, come into being through each other, for in the space defined by their reciprocal difference lies the poetic act of *naming* that grounds or inaugurates (*stiftet*) their relation (*Verhältnis*). The place of the poet is therefore always *in between*: his language institutes measure and establishes proportion, mediating between gods and mortals, bringing about a reconciliation of opposites in which, as Hölderlin learned from his study of Greek philosophy, part coincides with whole (ἕν καὶ πᾶν, the one and all), and unity corresponds to diversity (ἕν διαφέρον ἑαυτῷ, the one differentiated in itself).

The marriage of contraries, however, remains throughout Hölderlin's work a precarious, and utopian, synthesis. The apocalyptic conjuncture of heaven and earth is something that can only be experienced in memory or in anticipation, for it is an event no longer and not yet possible, located either in the mythical Golden Age of beginnings or in the Parousia that lies at time's end. The order of *history*, by contrast, teaches something quite different: God is Dead.[4] In "Patmos," his greatest medita-

[3] See M. H. Abrams, *Natural Supernaturalism: Tradition and Revolution in Romantic Literature* (New York, 1971), and Cyrus Hamlin, "The Poetics of Self-Consciousness in European Romanticism: Hölderlin's *Hyperion* and Wordsworth's *Prelude*," *Genre* 6, no. 2 (June 1973).

[4] Though Hölderlin distinguishes between "God" (Father Aether, Zeus the

tion on the *deus absconditus*, Hölderlin witnesses (well before Nietzsche) the terrifying withdrawal of divine presence from the world as Christ, last of the ancient gods, abandons his disciples to a diaspora of darkness and devastation:

> But when he dies,
> To whom beauty
> So adhered that his person
> Was a miracle, designated
> By the gods, and when they forever become
> Enigmas to each other, and elude each
> Other's grasp, they who lived in common
> Memory of him, and when sand
> And willows are blown away, and temples
> Are destroyed, when the honor
> Of the demigod and his disciples
> Is scattered to the winds and even
> The Almighty averts
> His face, leaving nothing
> Immortal to be seen in the sky
> Or on green earth, what is this?

If the heavens are now desolate, it is because a double estrangement has taken place: just as man has forgotten his love for God, so God has ostracized man, leaving him to wander through the night like an orphan. And yet, by a paradox of negative theology, the disappearance of God may be his most mysterious gift: as Hölderlin tersely observes in his poem "The Poet's Vocation,"

Thunderer, the Almighty or Most High, a remote and often wrathful sky-god) and "the gods" (*die Himmlischen*, the celestials or heavenly ones), the distance between singular and plural is far from absolute, indicating an open sweep of theological possibility that includes both polytheism and monotheism, both paganism and Christianity, as well as their eventual reconciliation. Broader contexts are provided by J. Hillis Miller, *The Disappearance of God: Five Nineteenth-Century Writers* (Cambridge, 1963), and Eugenio Donato, "Divine Agonies: Of Representation and Narrative in Romantic Poetics," *Glyph* 6 (Baltimore, 1979). Elinor Shaffer's *"Kubla Khan" and the Fall of Jerusalem: The Mythological School in Biblical Criticism and Secular Literature 1770–1880* (Cambridge, 1975), contains useful pages on "Patmos."

Gottes Fehl hilft ("God's lack helps"). In the new dispensation brought about by the death of God the poet's role is no longer to receive the fire from on high and offer it on in song to his fellow men; instead, he has now become the guardian of the empty intersection that defines the mutual infidelity of gods and mortals. In this silent locus his words now discover their source.

But the very concealment or hiddenness (*Verborgenheit*) of the divine, as Heidegger's commentaries on Hölderlin darkly suggest, defines the ground for its disclosure. Radiant by his very occlusion, God reveals himself by taking veil:

> God wears guises for man's sake.
> And hides his face from recognitions
> And veils the breezes with art.
> And time and air conceal
> His awesomeness, lest he be loved
> Too much in soul
> Or prayer.   ("Greece")

The distance of God, then, is integral to his proximity; he is, in the celebrated opening phrase of "Patmos," at once "Near and / Hard to grasp." Or, from a slightly different perspective, the absence of God may be said to establish his presence—which is why Hölderlin tends to conceive of man's relation to the divine in terms of the sign (*Zeichen*). For if the sign may be defined as the compound of a presence (the "signifier") and an absence (the "signified"), then the very disappearance of God as ultimate ground or guarantor of meaning enables poetry to become conscious of the radical dispossession—and the vertiginous autonomy—of its own discourse. Hölderlin's poetics of absence prefigures the supreme fictions of a Mallarmé or a Stevens in which "Poetry / Exceeding music must take the place / Of empty heaven and its hymns."

"He does not speak, he does not hide, he only gives signs," says Heraclitus of the Apollo of Delphi. The poet, too, is a maker of signs (*ein Zeigender*); and all signs express relation. Man, for example, is a sign:

A sign we are, without meaning
Without pain we are and have nearly
Lost our language in foreign lands . . .   ("Mnemosyne")

God is a sign:

His sign
Is silent in the thundering sky.   ("Patmos")

Everything therefore hinges on interpretation (*deuten*):

To keep God pure and maintain distinctions
Is entrusted us
Lest, and much depends
On this, penitence or a misconstrued
Sign
Bring down his judgment.   ("The Vatican . . .")

But the enigma of the sign lies not merely in language's capacity
to mean, or to refer, or to signify, but, more crucially, in the
mysterious fact that language (and hence man) can *be* at all—
hence Heidegger's repeated insistence on the ontological impli-
cations of Hölderlin's poetics. As an activity of *naming*, poetry
does not so much imitate or represent or symbolize something
beyond or prior to itself, but simply *says*, and, in so doing, estab-
lishes a site where what is said is all that lasts.[5]

daß gepfleget werde
Der veste Buchstab, und bestehendes gut
Gedeutet.   ("Patmos")

The act of translation demands, on the one hand, that one

[5] See George Steiner, *Heidegger* (New York, 1980), pp. 143-146. Heidegger's
essays on Hölderlin, "Remembrance of the Poet" and "Hölderlin and the Essence
of Poetry," may be found in his *Existence and Being*, ed. Werner Broch (Chicago,
1949). "What Are Poets For" and ". . . Poetically Man Dwells . . . " are contained
in Heidegger's *Poetry, Language, Thought*, trans. Albert Hofstadter (New York,
1971). Further commentary is contained in *Martin Heidegger and the Question of
Literature: Toward a Postmodern Literary Hermeneutics*, ed. William V. Spanos
(Bloomington, 1979), and Andrzej Warminski, " 'Patmos': The Senses of Inter-
pretation," *MLN* 91, no. 3 (April 1976).

venture out from one's native speech to take up residence in a foreign tongue and, on the other, that one accompany alien words home and provide them hospitality in a new local idiom. It is an activity that involves an asymptotic desire for a closeness that now and then (the gods willing) miraculously verges on complete fusion and at the same time entails an opposite impulse to take distance from the original, to retreat from the sheer otherness of its utterance. These two motions are antipodal and, in a sense, irreconcilable. Yet they are also profoundly reciprocal and, as Hölderlin believed, perhaps ultimately and precariously the same. The particular proportion that emerges when such antitheses are held in balance is akin to what he termed "measure" (*Maaß*). And measure, he felt, was precisely what all poetry was called to establish: a finding of relation, a delimiting of identity and difference, a process of exchange—in short, cognate to translation.

Hölderlin undertook his first major translation, a prose version of the first two books of the *Iliad*, at age sixteen; subsequent translations included Lucan's *Pharsalia*, as well as selections from Horace, Vergil, and Ovid (significantly enough, he chose to render the fable of Phaethon from the *Metamorphoses*). Hölderlin's most significant work as a translator, however, revolved around his ever-deepening dialogue with the Greeks. His prosodic experiments with the choruses of Sophocles dated back to 1796, and over the course of the next eight years he would continue to refine his versions of *Oedipus* and *Antigone*, accentuating (as he put it in an 1803 letter) the "Oriental" vitality of the tragedies, while at the same time "rectifying" what he considered to be some of their "aesthetic flaws." Hölderlin evidently hoped for a performance of his versions on the German stage but was greatly disappointed by the reception accorded his *Trauerspiele des Sophokles* upon their publication in 1804. Schelling, for one, saw them as further proof of his friend's "obvious derangement," and at least one reviewer sarcastically dismissed them as poor satires upon the contemporary German public. They would have to wait until the early twentieth century to be fully appreciated.

Hölderlin's translations of Pindar in 1799 to 1800 roughly coincided with his work on Sophicles—although, unlike his versions of *Oedipus* and *Antigone*, his inspired renderings of the Epinician odes would not see print until edited by Norbert von Hellingrath in 1911. Hellingrath's reverent philological scrutiny of Hölderlin's *Pindarübertragungen* revealed what George Steiner has termed "the most exalted, enigmatic stance in the literature of translation," for by adhering so literally to the original, by cleaving so closely to the lexical and syntactical textures of the Greek—often at the expense of what would be commonly termed its meaning—Hölderlin had in effect managed to create a new language, situated at the outer limits of intelligibility, neither recognizably Greek nor German, antique or modern, but located in a liminal zone somewhere in between.[6] Hölderlin proceeded in the belief that this visionary strategy of translation—whose humble word-for-word fidelity to the letter of the original paradoxically entailed a violent appropriation of its spirit—might succeed in revealing the ultimate etymological root (or *logos*) that lay buried beneath all the divisions of language. Yet he also remained keenly conscious of the fundamental hubris of his enterprise: How, given the essential limitation and fragmentation of human speech, could the translator aspire to disclose the unity of the divine Word? The pressures this awareness exerted on Hölderlin's language account for its extraordinary intensity and fragility. As Walter Benjamin observed in "The Task of the Translator," Hölderlin's translations forever skirt a bottomless abyss of silence—or madness.

The translation of Greece into Germany—this had always been a central ambition of Hölderlin's poetics. His early verse, composed under the twin influence of Klopstock and Schiller, had made use of a variety of quasi-classical strophic forms and measures, and by 1796 he had begun perfecting a domesticated Ger-

[6] See George Steiner's valuable discussion of Hölderlin as a translator in *After Babel: Aspects of Language and Translation* (New York, 1975), pp. 323-335. Steiner in turn builds on Walter Benjamin's "The Task of the Translator," in *Illuminations*, ed. Hannah Arendt (New York, 1969).

man version of the Asclepiadean and Alcaic stanza to complement his subsequent experiments with elegiac distichs in such major poems as "Brot und Wein" (1800–1801). His translations of Pindar in turn pointed toward new formal possibilities. In late 1799 he undertook "Wie Wenn am Feiertage" ("As on a Feastday"), an ambitious attempt to imitate the metrical and strophic structure of the Pindaric ode (or "hymnus," as Hölderlin tended to term it). The poem was a failure, largely because the transposition of Pindar's intricate patterns of metrical responsion only succeeded in cluttering its tempo; divorced from the dance that accompanied and reinforced the design of the Pindaric original, the shape of the hymn was simply too involved to be readily seized by the ear. Though Hölderlin would accordingly abandon the detailed reproduction of Pindar's metrical scheme in favor of freer rhythms (derived in part from his translations of Sophocles' choruses), he would nevertheless retain in his later hymns the overall triadic construction of the Pindaric ode, that is, its progression from strophe to antistrophe to epode—a form perfectly suited to the dialectical cast of Hölderlin's vision and one that he further refined through an elaborate theory of the "modulation of tones" (see the notes to "The Rhine," p. 259).

Hölderlin's adaptation of the triadic pattern of the Pindaric ode emphasized the strophe over the individual metrical unit as the constitutive structural element of the poem, with the result that enjambment became a device crucial to the swift cumulation of line upon line into whole:

> I have heard
> Of Elis and Olympia, have
> Stood atop Parnassos
> And above the mountains of the Isthmos
> And over toward
> Smyrna and down
> By Ephesos have I walked . . .   ("The Only One")

At its most effective such enjambment can create a vertiginous forward sweep, a virtual cascade of lines in which individual syllables are borne along in the great plunge of sound without, in the process, losing their own definition. Since the lines of Hölderlin's late hymns vary considerably in length and accentuation, they have looked to many twentieth-century readers like free verse—though as a rule they tend to follow a rising pattern in which the beginning of each line catches, with one or two unstressed syllables, the rhythmic swell of the preceding line and then goes on to gather accent as it proceeds:

> By the figtree
> My Achilles died,
> And Ajax lies
> By the grottoes of the sea,
> By streams, with Skamandros as neighbor.

("Mnemosyne")

Hölderlin's sense of cadence is perhaps only equaled by Wordsworth among his contemporaries; and just as Milton lies behind the ample periods of *The Prelude*, so Klopstock—and Pindar—inform Hölderlin's mastery of the phrasal unit, whether this be compressed into dense gnomic utterances of four or five words, or extended over a dozen lines through the various loops and leaps of a syntax whose idiosyncrasies are as notorious as Mallarmé's. Though Hölderlin's radical hyperbata and inversions are feasible in a language such as German (or Greek), where inflection, rather than word order, acts as the ultimate guarantor of grammatical intelligibility, it is virtually impossible to reproduce such syntax in English without falling into an idiom that recalls Milton at his most stilted.[7] In my translations I have therefore tried to convey the particular syntactical torque of Hölderlin's late hymns through means more native to American

---

[7] M. B. Benn's *Hölderlin and Pindar* (The Hague, 1962) cites Milton's rendering of Horace's *ridentem dicere verum/Quid vetat* ("Laughing to teach the truth/ What hinders") as an example of this particular strategy of translation. Ezra Pound's essay on "Early Translators of Homer," in *Literary Essays*, ed. T. S. Eliot (New York, 1968), contains much that is pertinent to the problem of translating Hölderlinian word order into English. I am also indebted to the example of the Fitts-Fitzgerald version of Sophocles' *Oedipus Cycle* (New York, 1949).

cadence. My primary ambition has been to retain the overall profile of the phrase while rendering what Hölderlin sometimes termed the "rhythm of representation," that is, the pace at which verbal relations come to be perceived.

By playing quick shifts of line and phrase against the architectonic stolidity of the strophe, Hölderlin manages to impart both velocity and mass to his hymns. A somewhat similar effect is created by the way his diction blends, without violation of decorum, solemnity and earthiness, classical or biblical elevation and homely Swabian proverbiality. Aware, as he notes in a late draft, that "The German tongue/Will not please the ear," Hölderlin nevertheless defends his vernacular in his hymn "To the Madonna":

> Yet, heavenly one, I will
> Sing your praise, and let no one
> Reproach the beauty
> Of my homegrown speech
> As I go to the fields
> Alone, where the lily
> Grows wild, without fear . . .

Though something of the *tone* of Hölderlin's voice can be carried over into American idiom, it is far more difficult to capture the precise resonances of many of his words, virtual echo chambers in which Swabian regionalisms ricochet off Lutheran German and Dorian or Attic Greek. One of Hölderlin's most striking habits of language involves the *figura etymologica*, an archeological trope that inscribes the word into origins, thereby revealing its ultimate grounding in metaphor. Thus the adjective *heilig* ("holy"), so essential to Hölderlin's poetic lexicon, has roots in *heil* ("whole," "heal"), just as the verb *denken* ("think") inevitably carries overtones of *danken* ("thank") and *gedenken* ("bear in mind," "recollect")—all of which, as Heidegger has shown, vibrate through the hymn "Andenken" ("Remembrance"). Much of this obviously escapes translation. How, for example, can "spirit" or "mind" render Hölderlin's etymological perception of *Geist* (he probably pronounced it "Geischt") as a kind of effervescence or pneumatic foam (*Gest/Gischt*) created by the fermentation of wine? How convey the implications of a private coinage such as *das Schickliche* (see notes to "The Ister"), or do justice to the seminal pun on Rhein (the river) and *rein* ("pure")?

There are instances, moreover, when Hölderlin's words only take on their full texture when read in the light of Greek. His frequent usage of the adverb *nemlich* ("namely") and the conjunction *aber* ("but") throughout the late hymns reflects the elusive nuances of the Greek particles *gar*, *men*, and *de*: depending on context, their meaning can range from the adversative ("but" or "yet"), to the explanatory ("for" or "because"), to the conjunctive ("and"); in certain cases they may simply serve to define a rhythmic (rather than strictly logical) relation between clauses.[8] The second sentence of "Remembrance" runs:

> *But* go now and greet
> The lovely Garonne
> And the gardens of Bordeaux,
> There, where the path cuts
> Along the shore and the stream dives
> Riverward, *but* a noble pair
> Of oaks and white poplars
> Looks on from above;
>
> All this still comes to mind and how
> The broad tops of elms
> Bend over the mill,
> *But* a figtree is growing in the courtyard.

Does the "but" (*aber*) here signify opposition or qualification? Or does it merely indicate a punctuative pause between different phrasal units? A late hymnic draft provides an extreme example

---

[8] See Frank Nisetich's introduction to his translations of Pindar's *Victory Songs* (Baltimore, 1980) for an excellent discussion of the intricate decisions the Greek particle demands of its translator.

of the way in which Hölderlin deploys these articles at once to conjoin and fracture the different angles of a single prismatic train of thought. The result almost suggests the multiple perspectives of cubism:

> *But* the paths
> Are evil. *For* like horses,
> The captive elements
> And ancient laws
> Of the earth go astray. *Yet* always
> The longing to reach beyond bounds. *But* much
> To be retained. *And* loyalty a must.
> *But* we shall not look forward
> Or back. Let ourselves rock, as
> On a boat, lapped by waves.   ("The fruits are ripe . . .")

In an influential essay on Hölderlin's late poetry Theodor Adorno has defined its most outstanding stylistic feature as *parataxis*, that is, the juxtaposition, without explanatory connectives, of various syntactical and grammatical elements (as opposed to *hypotaxis*, the subordination or coordination of phrase or clause). The increasingly paratactic character of Hölderlin's work from 1803 onward not only imparts an aura of urgency to his verse (in the onrush of vision there is simply no time to stop and explain) but also contributes to its difficulty, since the reader is left with the task of filling in the resultant blanks:

> John. Christ. Let me sing
> Of the latter as of Hercules or
> The island, bounded by cool ocean waters,
> Which held and rescued Peleus, refreshment
> After the wide desert of waves. But this
> Doesn't work. A fate rings differently. More wonderful.
> Richer to sing. The myth is
> Unfathomable ever since Him. And now
> Let me sing the journey of the knights
> To Jerusalem, and Heinrich wandering

In pain at Canossa. Let
My courage not abandon me. But first,
We must grasp this. Names are as the morning breeze
Ever since Christ. Become dreams. Fall, like error,
Upon the heart, and can kill if you do not
Weigh what they are, and understand.

("Patmos [Fragments of a later version]")

Edwin Muir remarked that this passage reads like something out of late Rilke, and Michael Hamburger has followed up on this insight in a valuable discussion of Hölderlin's pertinence to the poetics of German Expressionism.[9] But the style of parataxis, as Auerbach's *Mimesis* reminds us, is as ancient as it is modern: Hölderlin only seems so *new* because he has traveled so far back to poetry's most archaic roots. Norbert von Hellingrath was perhaps the first to demonstrate that Hölderlin's late hymns, far from constituting an aberration, rejoin the tradition of "austere harmony" as defined by Dionysius of Halicarnassus in reference to Homer, Pindar, Alcaeus, and Sophocles:

> It requires that the words should be like columns firmly planted and placed in strong positions, so that each word should be seen on every side, and that the parts should be at appreciable distances from one another, being separated by perceptible intervals. It does not in the least shrink from using frequently harsh sound-clashings which jar on the ear; like blocks of building stone that are laid together unworked, blocks that are not square and smooth, but preserve their natural roughness and irregularity.[10]

If each word is to be visible from every side, the disposition of the space between or around words becomes of paramount

[9] See chapter "1912" in Michael Hamburger's *Contraries: Studies in German Literature* (New York, 1970).
[10] W. Rhys Roberts' translation, quoted in M. B. Benn, *Hölderlin and Pindar*. See also D. S. Carne-Ross, *Instaurations: Essays in and out of Literature, Pindar to Pound* (Berkeley, 1979), pp. 29-60.

importance to the construction of the poem. Hölderlin, no less than Mallarmé, is a master of an interstitial design which demands of its translator that he render not merely the words on the page but, perhaps more crucially, the silences that zone them. Though it is difficult, given the state of Hölderlin's manuscripts, to speak of any definitive typographical layout of the page, it is nevertheless clear that in his work from 1803 onward the configuration of gaps and breaches becomes increasingly important to the rhythm of representation:

> But now even poor places
> Are in flower.
> And will rise
> Majestic.
> Mountain overhangs   lake,
> Warm   deep   but breezes cool
> Islands and peninsulas,
> Grottoes for praying,
>
> A sparkling shield,
> And quick, as roses . . .   ("But when the gods . . .")

To open the poem up to these kinds of intervals is to practice an aesthetic of the fragment. It is largely irrelevant whether the texts that his editors have labeled *Hymnische Entwürfe* ("Drafts of Hymns") or *Bruchstücke* ("Fragments") were indeed actually intended by Hölderlin to stand as self-sufficient entities: what matters is that *we* read them that way. Take the following poem:

> I want to build
>
> and raise new
> the temple of Theseus and the stadiums
> and where Perikles lived
>
> But there's no money, too much spent
> today. I had a guest
> over   and we sat together

Though this may indeed be a "fragment," it is in no sense incomplete. Nothing could be added or subtracted from the text without utterly destroying its perfect economy.[11]

To the twentieth-century reader whose taste has been shaped by *The Waste Land* and *The Cantos*, Hölderlin's late drafts and fragments may well be the most accessible portion of his oeuvre, precisely because they seem most modern. As Friedrich Schlegel observed in one of his *Athenäums-Fragmente* (1798): "Many works of the Ancients have become fragments. Many works of the Moderns are fragments the moment they come into being." But Hölderlin's fragments, as Schlegel's aphorism implies, are modern only to the extent that they take on the same face that antiquity wears to us: headless torsos, shards of vases, broken columns, scattered traces:

> Cities of the Euphrates,
> Streets of Palmyra,
> Columns wooding the desert plain,
> What are you?   ("Ages of Life")

Voleny's *Les Ruines, ou méditations sur les révolutions des empires* (1791) supplied Hölderlin (and later Byron and Shelley) with the topos: the modern imagination invents itself (and thereby reinvents antiquity) out of the evidence of wreckage; it has only fragments to shore against its ruins. The eloquent debris of Pal-

---

[11] Since almost nothing of Hölderlin's work between 1801 and 1806 was published in his own lifetime, it is of course difficult to construe his ultimate intentions. One of the last poems he saw into print, however, was "Half of Life" (published in 1805 with eight other *Nightsongs*). Hölderlin's realization that this brief text—originally a fragmentary outgrowth of the hymn "As on a Feastday"—could stand on its own as an independent poem would seem to corroborate his evolving conception of form. As Hamburger points out in *Contraries*, "Half of Life" anticipates the poetics of Imagism by a century. Hölderlin wrote Böhlendorff in the fall of 1802: "I think we shall not simply provide a commentary on the poets up to our times, but that the style of poetry [*Sangart*] will take on an altogether different character, and that the reason we are not in fashion is because, for the first time since the Greeks, we are again beginning to sing in a national and natural, that is, truly original, manner." Hölderlin, in other words, was quite conscious of the essential modernity of his poetic project. His concern with the modalities of fragmentation is shared by Wordsworth and Coleridge; see Thomas McFarland, *Romanticism and the Forms of Ruin* (Princeton, 1981).

myra or Herculaneum finds its philological equivalent in the miscellaneous scraps of Pindar that Hölderlin translated from Estienne's Renaissance edition sometime between 1803 and 1805. Hölderlin's commentaries on these *membra disjecta* of Pindar constitute a series of meditations on ruins or, more precisely, a sequence of reflections on the nature of hermeneutic activity per se, for to scrutinize a fragment is to move from the presence of a part to the absence of the whole, to seize upon the sign as witness of something that is forever elsewhere—in a past that is no longer, or in a future that has yet to be born.

Hölderlin's late drafts and fragments demand a similar interpretive engagement on the part of the reader, for they are above all works in progress, neither beginnings nor endings but becomings. Until recently, editions of Hölderlin tended to ignore the radically open and processual character of his poetry. By proposing "authoritative" readings of his texts, such scholars as Friederich Beissner, editor of the monumental *Grosse Stuttgarter Ausgabe* of Hölderlin's complete works (1943–1972), created the misleading impression that definitive versions of the poems could exist. Hölderlin's manuscripts, especially those of his unpublished work between 1800 and 1806, are veritable palimpsests, which require the patience of a paleographer to dicipher. Textual strata of different dates lie superimposed upon each other, at times barely legible, fault lines suddenly interrupt a phrase; rich lodes of image tail off into margins often crowded with outcroppings of revision. Given their verbal imbrication, definitive readings of these manuscripts become virtually impossible: the editor finds himself not simply reproducing but instead constituting—and thereby inventing—the text at hand. Whereas previous editions of Hölderlin had more or less masked this authorial (and authoritarian) role of the editor, the so-called Frankfurt Edition currently in progress under the direction of D. E. Sattler challenges the sovereign procedures of traditional Hölderlin scholarship by inviting the reader to participate in the generation of the text. Sattler first gives a photographic reproduction of the manuscript, followed by a diplomatic copy that transcribes the spatial configuration of the original. This is in turn succeeded by a "phase analysis," which converts the spatial disposition of the page into a temporal sequence whose various stages of composition are indicated by different typefaces. Only at the end of this process is there finally printed a provisional version of the poem, or "reading text."

What emerges from this new Frankfurt Edition, then, is not a closed canon of inert textual artifacts but rather a mapping of poems in process. There is no pretense of providing definitive or authoritative versions; instead, the layerings and discontinuities of the texts are reproduced to allow for the proliferation of possible readings. And herein lie the political implications of this edition, published, significantly enough, under the maverick Marxist imprint of the Roter Stern Verlag. By presenting Hölderlin's texts as events rather than objects, as processes rather than products, it converts the reader from passive consumer into active participant in the genesis of the poem, while at the same time calling attention to the fundamentally historical character of both the reader's and writer's activity.[12] Wherever feasible I have based my translations on the "reading texts" proposed by Sattler: a rendering of the complete variorum edition remains, for the moment, a utopian prospect and, moreover, the full publication of Hölderlin's late work by Roter Stern still lies several years off. Although therefore unable to follow the letter of the Frankfurt Edition, I have at least tried to observe its spirit. In many respects the translator of Hölderlin finds himself in the same position as his editor: he deciphers what appears to occur before his eyes and ears, he interprets, he commits himself to a pattern of decision, and in the end produces a poem that can only stand as provisional.

[12] See Helen Fehevary, *Hölderlin and the Left* (Heidelberg, 1977), pp. 233-239, and the appendix to Rainer Nägele's essay on "Stimme des Volks," *Glyph* 5 (Baltimore, 1979).

Allda bin ich
Alles miteinander. ("Vom Abgrund nemlich . . .")

Although Hölderlin scholarship traditionally designates his late work in free rhythms as *Hymns* or *Drafts of Hymns*, Hölderlin's own working title seems to have been *vaterländische Gesänge*. To translate this as "patriotic songs" or "songs of the Fatherland," however, is immediately to conjure up the worst kitsch of German nationalism—*Wandervögel* strenuously exulting in the complacencies of the homeland. And indeed it was very much in this fashion that Hölderlin came to be misunderstood during the Third Reich. Officially consecrated as the rhapsode of Germanic destiny, recited to the Führer on his fiftieth birthday, gnomically explicated by Martin Heidegger, issued to soldiers in a special 1943 "field edition" prepared under the joint auspices of the Hölderlin Society and the Nazi Cultural Ministry, Hölderlin became the literary property of the mystagogues of *Kultur*. If Hölderlin was again to become readable to the post-war generation, his name had to be cleansed of the Nazi stain to which Gunter Eich's 1948 poem "Latrine" succinctly alluded with a provocative rhyme on "Hölderlin" and "urine."

Through the work of Pierre Bertaux and a number of younger German scholars a new image of the poet began to take shape by the mid-sixties. In the place of the noble patriotic bard canonized by the brown-shirts there emerged a left-wing Hölderlin, bitter critic of German provincialism, reader of Rousseau, partisan of the French Revolution, and member of secret Jacobin societies in his native Swabia. The *succès de scandale* of Peter Weiss's 1971 *Hölderlin* did much to popularize this revisionist version of the poet. Explicitly underscoring Hölderlin's radical legacy, Weiss closed his play with an apocryphal scene in which the young Karl Marx comes to pay homage to the mad prophet in his Tübingen tower and, in allegorical rite of passage, apostolically receives from him the revolutionary flame.

"I believe in a forthcoming revolution of attitudes and conceptions which will make everything that has gone before turn red with shame," Hölderlin wrote a friend in Paris in early 1797;

"And to this Germany can perhaps contribute a great deal." Hölderlin's late *vaterländische Gesänge* stem from the same chiliastic conviction that the gods will soon return to Germany— even though the bleak political realities of the Napoleonic Wars may for the moment cast doubt on the imminence of their homecoming:

> There was a secret
> Time when by nature I would have said
> They were coming to Germany. But now, since the earth
> Is like the sea, and the nations, like men who cannot
> Cross to each other's coasts, squabble
> Among themselves, I speak as follows . . .
>
> ("The Nearest the Best")

Hölderlin hoped for nothing less than a political or imaginative apocalypse that would herald a new civilization, a universal resurrection in a restored paradise such as Blake prophesies at the conclusion of *Jerusalem*, or Shelley celebrates with the union of Prometheus and Asia in the final act of *Prometheus Unbound*. Like Wordsworth, Hölderlin believed that this Eternal Day would dawn

> Not in Utopia,—subterranean fields,—
> Of some secreted island, Heaven knows where!
> But in the very world, which is the world
> Of all of us,—the place where, in the end,
> We find our happiness or not at all!
>
> (*The Prelude*, Book XI, ll. 140–144)

A *paradiso terrestre*, here, in the present tense, on German ground— this is the site Hölderlin defines as the Fatherland. It is a place not unlike Whitman's America:

> and you gather me, O
> Flowers of Germany, O my heart turns
> Into unerring crystal, touchstone
> Of light when   Germany
>
> ("We set out from the abyss . . .")

To sing the Fatherland is to conceive poetry above all as an act of praise, as a public declaration of astonishment and gratitude in which "the world's native produce, as it meets/The sense with less habitual stretch of mind,/Is pondered as a miracle" (Wordsworth). Drawing upon a tradition that reaches back to include the Homeric hymns and Pindar's odes, as well as the psalms and canticles of Protestant worship, Hölderlin accordingly defines the poet as one who leads the *polis* (or the congregation) in choric celebration of its heroes and gods:

> O fellow poets, we must take it upon ourselves
> To stand, heads bared, beneath the tempests
> Of the Lord, and seize the Father's lightning
> With our hands, and offer the people
> This gift of heaven, veiled in song. ("As on a Feastday")

Occupying a privileged space between the fiery heavens and the earthly community, the poet not only solemnizes the manifestations of the divine but is also called upon to translate or mediate these to his fellow men. To praise is always to interpret, that is, to establish measure among men (and hence to institute community) while articulating the necessary proportions that gods and mortals must respectively observe. Everything depends on balance: unmeasured praise is as dangerous as despair. Between these two poles—between the hymnic celebration of plenitude and the elegiac lamentation of loss—Hölderlin's *vaterländische Gesänge* maintain a precarious equilibrium.

The objects of Hölderlin's praise are various. He celebrates demigods (Dionysus, Hercules, Christ), classical heroes (Achilles, Ajax, Oedipus), Christian saints (the apostle John and John of Patmos), world historical figures (Frederick Barbarossa, Columbus, Rousseau)—all of them "Giant Forms" whose various destinies, if interpreted correctly, become signs of the ways of God among men and, to that extent, illuminate the fate that awaits the Fatherland. Hölderlin's greatest poetry of praise, however, is devoted to Nature, for it is in the immediate features of landscape that he discerns the most compelling evidence of divine process. Upon returning to Nürtingen in the fall of 1802, he writes to Böhlendorff:

> The more I study nature here around home, the more I am moved by it. The thunderstorm, perceived not only in its most extreme manifestation but precisely as a power and figure among the various other forms of the sky, the light, active as a principle and resembling fate, working to impart national shape so that we might possess something sacred, the urgency of its comings and goings, the particular character of the forests, and the way in which the diversities of nature all converge in one area, so that all the holy places of the earth come together in a single place, and the philosophical light around my window— all this is now my joy. Let me not forget how I have come this far!

The exact physiognomy of the sky, the workings of the light, the intuition of locality as a field of convergences, as a place where differences are gathered—all these are lessons of travel. Hölderlin had gone abroad to discover his native ground. He learned in the process that the fundamental site of poetry is always local (or "national," or *vaterländisch*) and, more importantly, that the local defines a space in which "all the holy places of the earth come together in a single place." To be truly *here* is to be everywhere; any locus is potentially an *omphalos*. Frankfurt, for example, the site of Diotima's grave, is

> the navel
> Of this earth, and this age
> Is time of German fusion.
> A wild hill looms over the slope
> Of my gardens. Cherry trees. And sharp breath blows
> Through rock's holes. Here I am everything
> At once.   ("We set out from the abyss . . .")

In an early essay "On Religion" Hölderlin defined the "mythic" as a dialectical synthesis of the local and the universal, of the particular and the general, of the concrete and the abstract. The geography of his late hymns is "mythic" in a similar sense. Just as a poem like "Patmos" telescopes past, present, and future into a single expanse of vision, so his native Swabia, the Aegean island of Patmos, and biblical Palestine are all topographically overlaid into a single site in the course of the hymn. For Hölderlin, writing was a mode of mapping—legend has it that the walls of his room were covered with maps of the four quarters of the earth. One of the major themes of his sprawling poem, "Columbus," is the power of the imagination to discover a New World, thereby causing a radical revision of all previous cartography:

> [voyages of discovery
> as attempts to define
> the Hesperidean orbis as
> against that of the ancients] . . .

In the *orbis novus* of Hölderlin's late hymns and fragments time and space are abolished at the break of the new Hesperidean Day. Geography takes on the face of eternity: streams rush through Scotland toward the lakes of Lombardy, the landscape of Provence melds with the hills of Bavaria, dawn pours into Swabia from Asia, and the Danube carries coolness to the Black Sea. Hölderlin's landscapes are most frequently imagined as a pattern of vectors or moving energies: paths through mountain passes, bridges over abysses, the course of rivers or winds, the track of the sun from east to west, the flight of migratory birds—all trace a process of becoming, a motion at once toward and away from the source.

Landscape may also be read as a network of relations. Hölderlin writes to a friend in 1804 about a forthcoming volume of picturesque *Views of the Rhine*:

> I am curious to see how they come out; whether they will be lifted from nature purely and simply, so that nothing extraneous or uncharacteristic be included on either side

and the earth hold itself in good balance with the sky, so that the light which marks [*bezeichnet*] this balance in its particular proportion [*Verhältnis*] not be crooked or produce a charming illusion. Much depends on the internal angle of the artwork and on its external frame.

The prospects of Hölderlin's hymns are designed with a similar eye for ratio and rhyme: heights balanced with depths, mountains mirrored in lakes, Father Aether coupled with Mother Earth. And light is the sign of this equilibrium, the visible messenger of interchange:

> But when
> The sacred light slants through
> The play of breezes and the spirit
> Of joy glides down to earth
> On cooler beams, the deer succumbs, unaccustomed
> To such beauty, and slumbers in a waking sleep
> Before the stars draw near.
>   ("At the Source of the Danube")

The course of the Rhine or the Danube embodies another series of proportions, at once horizontal and vertical, spatial and temporal, for in the struggle between river and bank, nature and culture, inception and accomplishment, origin and fate, a measure is established that bespeaks the dialogue of earth and sky, men and gods:

> There is a reason rivers run
> Through dry land. But how? All that is needed
> Is a sign, pure and simple, which bears
> Sun and moon in mind, indivisible,
> And goes its way night and day, and
> The gods will feel each other's warmth.
> Which is why rivers
> Are the Almighty's joy. How could He otherwise
> Descend?   ("The Ister")

Hölderlin's ideal landscape is always theophanic, a scripture to be reverently read and interpreted, a radiant figuration of divine design.[13]

Such visionary topography, however, does not exclude a precise attention to the minute particulars of the *genius loci*, whatever their local habitation or their name:

> And Stuttgart where I,
> Creature of the moment,
> Could lie buried,
> There, at the bend
> In the road and
>   near the Weinsteig
> Down where the town comes back
> Into hearing on the green valley floor,
> Quietly sounding through the apple trees . . .
>   ("Alps . . .")

As Christopher Middleton has finely observed,[14] Hölderlin is not only keenly sensitive to the oscillations of light (frequently expressed by the acute shimmer of the verb *glänzen*) but also deeply attuned to the vibrations of auditory phenomena that range from barely perceptible rustlings and rushings (*säuseln, rauschen*), through firmer resonances and echoings (*tönen, hallen*), to the ominous rumblings and thunderings that announce the approach of the divine. The intricate aural profiles of a poem like "Greece" are the acoustic equivalent of the inscapes of Hopkins:

> The clear tempered clouds
> Carry like the blackbird's call, well-
> Tuned by the thunder, by God being there.

---

[13] See Geoffrey Hartman, "Wordsworth, Inscriptions, and Romantic Nature Poetry" and "Romantic Poetry and Genius Loci," in *Beyond Formalism* (New Haven, 1970), and, from a different perspective, Paul de Man, "The Intentional Structure of the Romantic Image," in *Romanticism and Consciousness*, ed. Harold Bloom (New York, 1970).

[14] See the introduction to his *Selected Poems* of Hölderlin and Mörike (Chicago, 1972).

And cries ring out, as to catch sight
Of heroes and immortal life;
The memories are many. And
Vibrate, like a drumskin,
With all the ravages . . . from which
The earth proceeds . . .

To attend to such harmony is to discover an ultimate simplicity:

Would I like to be a comet? I think so.
They are swift as birds, they flower
With fire, childlike in purity. To desire
More than this is beyond human measure.

(In lovely blue . . .")

Nightsongs

Hälfte des Lebens

Mit gelben Birnen hänget
Und voll mit wilden Rosen
Das Land in den See,
Ihr holden Schwäne,
Und trunken von Küssen
Tunkt ihr das Haupt
Ins heilignüchterne Wasser.

Weh mir, wo nehm' ich, wenn
Es Winter ist, die Blumen, und wo
Den Sonnenschein,
Und Schatten der Erde?
Die Mauern stehn
Sprachlos und kalt, im Winde
Klirren die Fahnen.

Half of Life

With its yellow pears
And wild roses everywhere
The shore hangs in the lake,
O gracious swans,
And drunk with kisses
You dip your heads
In the sobering holy water.

Ah, where will I find
Flowers, come winter,
And where the sunshine
And shade of the earth?
Walls stand cold
And speechless, in the wind
The weathervanes creak.

Der Winkel von Hahrdt

Hinunter sinket der Wald,
Und Knospen ähnlich, hängen
Einwärts die Blätter, denen
Blüht unten auf ein Grund,
Nicht gar unmündig
Da nemlich ist Ulrich
Gegangen; oft sinnt, über den Fußtritt,
Ein groß Schiksaal
Bereit, an übrigem Orte.

The Shelter at Hahrdt

The forest sinks off
And like buds, the leaves
Hang inward, to which
The valley floor below
Flowers up, far from mute,
For Ulrich passed through
These parts; a great destiny
Often broods over his footprint,
Ready, among the remains.

Lebensalter

Ihr Städte des Euphraths!
Ihr Gassen von Palmyra!
Ihr Säulenwälder in der Ebne der Wüste,
Was seid ihr?
Euch hat die Kronen,
Dieweil ihr über die Gränze
Der Othmenden seid gegangen,
Von Himmlischen der Rauchdampf und
Hinweg das Feuer genommen;
Jezt aber siz ich unter Wolken, darin
Ein jedes eine Ruh hat eigen, unter
Wohleingerichteten Eichen, auf
Der Haide des Rehs, und fremd
Erscheinen und gestorben mir
Der Seeligen Geister.

Ages of Life

Cities of the Euphrates,
Streets of Palmyra,
Columns wooding the desert plain,
What are you?
You were stripped of your crowns,
As you crossed beyond
The bounds of breath,
By the smoke
And fire of the gods;
But now I sit under clouds, in which
Each thing finds its peace, under
A fine stand of oaks, by
The deer meadow, and strange
And dead, they appear to me,
The spirits of the blest.

Hymns

Am Quell der Donau

Denn, wie wenn hoch von der herrlichgestimmten, der Orgel
Im heiligen Saal,
Reinquillend aus den unerschöpflichen Röhren,
Das Vorspiel, wekend, des Morgens beginnt
Und weitumher, von Halle zu Halle,
Der erfrischende nun, der melodische Strom rinnt,
Bis in den kalten Schatten das Haus
Von Begeisterungen erfüllt,
Nun aber erwacht ist, nun, aufsteigend ihr,
Der Sonne des Fests, antwortet
Der Chor der Gemeinde; so kam
Das Wort aus Osten zu uns,
Und an Parnassos Felsen und am Kithäron hör' ich
O Asia, das Echo von dir und es bricht sich
Am Kapitol und jählings herab von den Alpen

Kommt eine Fremdlingin sie
Zu uns, die Erwekerin,
Die menschenbildende Stimme.
Da faßt' ein Staunen die Seele
Der Getroffenen all und Nacht
War über den Augen der Besten.
Denn vieles vermag
Und die Fluth und den Fels und Feuersgewalt auch
Bezwinget mit Kunst der Mensch
Und achtet, der Hochgesinnte, das Schwerdt
Nicht, aber es steht
Vor Göttlichem der Starke niedergeschlagen,

Und gleichet dem Wild fast; das,
Von süßer Jugend getrieben,
Schweift rastlos über die Berg'

At the Source of the Danube

As when the prelude to morning wells forth
In church,
And the majestic stops of the organ
Overflow in a cascade of chords,
And the awakening melody streams
From room to room,
Quickening, inspiriting
Even the coldest shadows of the house,
And now stirring, now rising toward
The sun of celebration,
The congregation replies in chorus: so
The Word came down to us from the East,
And among the rocks of Parnassos and on Kithairon I hear
Your echo, Asia, breaking over
The Capitol and headlong down the Alps

She comes to us, this stranger
Who wakes us, this voice
Which makes us men.
And every soul thus struck
Was seized with awe, and night
Fell upon the eyes of the best.
For the powers of man
Are many, by his art
Flood, stone and fire are mastered,
Nor, high-minded, does he shy from
The sword, yet when faced
With the gods, the strong are laid low,

Almost like the deer who, driven
By his sweet youth,
Restlessly roves the mountains,

Und fühlet die eigene Kraft
In der Mittagshizze. Wenn aber
Herabgeführt, in spielenden Lüften,
Das heilige Licht, und mit dem kühleren Stral
Der freudige Geist kommt zu
Der seeligen Erde, dann erliegt es, ungewohnt
Des Schönsten und schlummert wachenden Schlaf,
Noch ehe Gestirn naht. So auch wir. Denn manchen erlosch
Das Augenlicht schon vor den göttlichgesendeten Gaben,

Den freundlichen, die aus Ionien uns,
Auch aus Arabia kamen, und froh ward
Der theuern Lehr' und auch der holden Gesänge
Die Seele jener Entschlafenen nie,
Doch einige wachten. Und sie wandelten oft
Zufrieden unter euch, ihr Bürger schöner Städte,
Beim Kampfspiel, wo sonst unsichtbar der Heros
Geheim bei Dichtern saß, die Ringer schaut und lächelnd
Pries, der gepriesene, die müßigernsten Kinder.
Ein unaufhörlich Lieben wars und ists.
Und wohlgeschieden, aber darum denken
Wir aneinander doch, ihr Fröhlichen am Isthmos,
Und am Cephyß und am Taygetos,
Auch eurer denken wir, ihr Thale des Kaukasos,
So alt ihr seid, ihr Paradiese dort
Und deiner Patriarchen und deiner Propheten,

O Asia, deiner Starken, o Mutter!
Die furchtlos vor den Zeichen der Welt,
Und den Himmel auf Schultern und alles Schiksaal,
Taglang auf Bergen gewurzelt,
Zuerst es verstanden,
Allein zu reden
Zu Gott. Die ruhn nun. Aber wenn ihr

Sensing his own strength
In the heat of noon. But when
The sacred light slants through
The play of breezes and the spirit
Of joy glides down to earth
On cooler beams, the deer succumbs, unaccustomed
To such beauty, and slumbers in a waking sleep
Before the stars draw near. Likewise with us. For the light
Went out in many eyes at the sight of those friendly,
      god-sent gifts

That came to us from Ionia
And Arabia, and those sleeping souls
Never knew the joy of
The precious teachings or gracious songs,
Though a few did remain awake. And often mingled
Contentedly with you, citizens of lovely towns, taking in
The Games where the Hero, invisible, would sit in secret
Among the poets, watching the wrestlers and with a smile
Praise (he, the bepraised) these children so gravely at play.
It was love without end. It still is.
And has parted ways. Which is why we think
Of each other, O joyous ones, on the Isthmos,
On Kephisos and Taygetos,
And think of you, O valleys of the Kaukasos,
Whatever your antiquity, paradises far,
And your patriarchs and prophets,

O Mother Asia, and your heroes
Without fear for the signs of the world,
Heaven and fate upon their shoulders,
Rooted on mountaintops days on end,
Were the first to understand
Speaking to God
Alone. These now rest. But since,

Und diß ist zu sagen,
Ihr Alten all, nicht sagtet, woher?
Wir nennen dich, heilggenöthiget, nennen,
Natur! dich wir, und neu, wie dem Bad entsteigt
Dir alles Göttlichgeborne.

Zwar gehn wir fast, wie die Waisen;
Wohl ists, wie sonst, nur jene Pflege nicht wieder;
Doch Jünglinge, der Kindheit gedenk,
Im Hauße sind auch diese nicht fremde.
Sie leben dreifach, eben wie auch
Die ersten Söhne des Himmels.
Und nicht umsonst ward uns
In die Seele die Treue gegeben.
Nicht uns, auch Eures bewahrt sie,
Und bei den Heiligtümern, den Waffen des Worts
Die scheidend ihr den Ungeschikteren uns
Ihr Schiksaalssöhne, zurükgelassen

Ihr guten Geister, da seid ihr auch,
Oftmals, wenn einen dann die heilige Wolk umschwebt,
Da staunen wir und wissens nicht zu deuten.
Ihr aber würzt mit Nectar uns den Othem
Und dann frohloken wir oft oder es befällt uns
Ein Sinnen, wenn ihr aber einen zu sehr liebt
Er ruht nicht, bis er euer einer geworden.
Darum, ihr Gütigen! umgebet mich leicht,
Damit ich bleiben möge, denn noch ist manches zu singen,
Jezt aber endiget, seeligweinend,
Wie eine Sage der Liebe,
Mir der Gesang, und so auch ist er
Mir, mit Erröthen, Erblassen,
Von Anfang her gegangen. Doch Alles geht so.

And mention must be made of this,
O ancients, since you would not say where
We draw your name, we are divinely compelled
To name you Nature, and every god-born thing
Emerges from you, fresh, newly bathed.

True, we almost make our way like orphans;
Much remains the same, though the tender care be forever lost;
But young men who remember childhood
Are no strangers to this house.
They live threefold, just like
The first sons of heaven.
Loyalty was not imparted
To our souls in vain. It preserves
Not us alone, but what is yours,
And in the holy relics, in the weapons of the Word
Which, O sons of fate, you left behind
For us, less fated, less skilled,

O friendly spirits, in these you are also present,
Often, when your holy cloud hovers round one of us,
We are seized with awe, unable to explain.
But when you spice our breath with nectar,
We rejoice or plunge
Into thought, yet if you love a man too much,
He has no peace until received in your company.
Therefore, O benevolent ones, enfold me lightly
And let me linger on, for there is still much to sing,
But now, weeping for joy,
Like a tale of love,
My song comes to its end, just as
The blush and blanch of it have been with me
From the start. But so things go.

Die Wanderung

Glükseelig Suevien, meine Mutter,
Auch du, der glänzenderen, der Schwester
Lombarda drüben gleich,
Von hundert Bächen durchflossen!
Und Bäume genug, weißblühend und röthlich,
Und dunklere, wild, tiefgrünenden Laubs voll
Und Alpengebirg der Schweiz auch überschattet
Benachbartes dich; denn nah dem Heerde des Haußes
Wohnst du, und hörst, wie drinnen
Aus silbernen Opferschaalen
Der Quell rauscht, ausgeschüttet
Von reinen Händen, wenn berührt

Von warmen Stralen
Krystallenes Eis und umgestürzt
Vom leichtanregenden Lichte
Der schneeige Gipfel übergießt die Erde
Mit reinestem Wasser. Darum ist
Dir angeboren die Treue. Schwer verläßt,
Was nahe dem Ursprung wohnet, den Ort.
Und deine Kinder, die Städte,
Am weithindämmernden See,
An Nekars Weiden, am Rheine,
Sie alle meinen, es wäre
Sonst nirgend besser zu wohnen.

Ich aber will dem Kaukasos zu!
Denn sagen hört' ich
Noch heut in den Lüften:
Frei sei'n, wie Schwalben, die Dichter.
Auch hat mir ohnediß
In jüngeren Tagen Eines vertraut,

The Migration

Blessed Swabia, my mother,
Traversed by a hundred brooks
Like Lombardy, your more luminous
Sister across the way,
And trees enough, with blossoms white and red,
And darker ones, growing wild, full of deep greens,
And the neighborly Swiss Alps
Provide you with shade; for your dwelling place is near
The hearth, and within you hear
The wellspring purl
From silver cups, pure hands
Pouring the libation, as the sun

Thaws ice-crystals and,
Avalanched
By the quickening light,
Snowcaps drench the earth
With the purest water. So loyalty
To origin is innate to you. A place of dwelling
This near the source is hard to leave.
And your offspring, the towns
By shimmering lakes,
By the Neckar's willows, by the Rhine,
All agree there is no
Better spot for home.

Yet I long for the Kaukasos!
Only today I heard
The breezes say
Poets are free as swallows.
And besides, I was told
Long ago that our forefathers,

Es seien vor alter Zeit
Die Eltern einst, das deutsche Geschlecht,
Still fortgezogen von Wellen der Donau
Am Sommertage, da diese
Sich Schatten suchten, zusammen
Mit Kindern der Sonn'
Am schwarzen Meere gekommen;
Und nicht umsonst sei diß
Das gastfreundliche genennet.

Denn, als sie erst angesehen,
Da nahten die Anderen erst; dann sazten auch
Die Unseren sich neugierig unter den Ölbaum.
Doch als sich ihre Gewande berührt,
Und keiner vernehmen konnte
Die eigene Rede des andern, wäre wohl
Entstanden ein Zwist, wenn nicht aus Zweigen herunter
Gekommen wäre die Kühlung,
Die Lächeln über das Angesicht
Der Streitenden öfters breitet, und eine Weile
Sahn still sie auf, dann reichten sie sich
Die Hände liebend einander. Und bald

Vertauschten sie Waffen und all
Die lieben Güter des Haußes,
Vertauschten das Wort auch und es wünschten
Die freundlichen Väter umsonst nichts
Beim Hochzeitjubel den Kindern.
Denn aus den heiligvermählten
Wuchs schöner, denn Alles,
Was vor und nach
Von Menschen sich nannt', ein Geschlecht auf. Wo,
Wo aber wohnt ihr, liebe Verwandten;
Daß wir das Bündniß wiederbegehn
Und der theuern Ahnen gedenken?

The German tribe, quietly
Coasted down the Danube
Of a summer's day
And reached the Black Sea,
Meeting with the children
Of the sun
Seeking shade.
Not for nothing
They call this sea Hospitable.

On first catching sight, it was the others
Who drew near; intrigued, our people
Joined them beneath the olive trees.
And as they grazed each other's garments
But cold not understand
Each other's speech, there would have
Been a fight, had not a cooling
Come down from the boughs
And spread a smile, as it often does,
Across belligerent faces; for a while
They stared in silence, then offered
Their hands in friendship. And soon

They traded weapons and all
Their precious household goods,
And exchanged the Word, and fathers
Saw that nothing lacked
At their children's wedding feasts.
And from these sacred unions
A race arose, more beautiful than anything
By the name of man
Before or since.
But where can I find you, dear kinsmen,
That we might recelebrate the vows
And honor the memory of our ancestors?

Dort an den Ufern, unter den Bäumen
Ionias, in Ebenen des Kaisters,
Wo Kraniche, des Aethers froh,
Umschlossen sind von fernhindämmernden Bergen;
Dort wart auch ihr, ihr Schönsten! oder pflegtet
Der Inseln, die mit Wein bekränzt,
Voll tönten von Gesang; noch andere wohnten
Am Tayget, am vielgepriesnen Himettos,
Die blühten zulezt; doch von
Parnassos Quell bis zu des Tmolos
Goldglänzenden Bächen erklang
Ein ewiges Lied; so rauschten
Damals die Wälder und all
Die Saitenspiele zusamt
Von himmlischer Milde gerühret.

O Land des Homer!
Am purpurnen Kirschbaum oder wenn
Von dir gesandt im Weinberg mir
Die jungen Pfirsiche grünen,
Und die Schwalbe fernher kommt und vieles erzählend
An meinen Wänden ihr Haus baut, in
Den Tagen des Mais, auch unter den Sternen
Gedenk' ich, o Ionia, dein! doch Menschen
Ist Gegenwärtiges lieb. Drum bin ich
Gekommen, euch, ihr Inseln, zu sehn, und euch,
Ihr Mündungen der Ströme, o ihr Hallen der Thetis,
Ihr Wälder, euch, und euch, ihr Wolken des Ida!

Doch nicht zu bleiben gedenk ich.
Unfreundlich ist und schwer zu gewinnen
Die Verschlossene, der ich entkommen, die Mutter.
Von ihren Söhnen einer, der Rhein,
Mit Gewalt wollt' er ans Herz ihr stürzen und schwand
Der Zurükgestoßene, niemand weiß, wohin, in die Ferne.

There on the shores, beneath the trees
Of Ionia, on the plains of the Cayster,
Where cranes delight in aether,
Bounded by the far-shimmering peaks,
You too were there, O beautiful ones! Or
Tilled islands, garlanded with vines,
Resounding with song; and others dwelt
By Taygetos, by fabled Hymettos,
And were the last to flower; yet from
The springs of Parnassos to Tmolos'
Gold-glimmering brooks, one everlasting
Hymn rang forth; and the forests
All rustled, every lyre
In unison
At heaven's gentle touch.

Land of Homer!
By the scarlet cherry tree, or when
The young peaches you sent to me
Are still green in the vineyard,
And the swallow arrives from afar and, bringing endless news,
Builds her house in my walls, in
Maytime, and under stars,
Ionia, I think of you. But since men
Are found of presences, I have come
To visit you, islands, and you,
O rivermouths, halls of Thetis,
And you, O woods, and you, O clouds over Ida!

Yet I do not think I'll linger long.
What I flee is cold and hard
To please, a mystery, my mother.
One of her sons, the Rhine, once tried
To take her heart by force, then disappeared
Into the distance, spurned, who knows where.

Doch so nicht wünscht' ich gegangen zu seyn,
Von ihr und nur, euch einzuladen,
Bin ich zu euch, ihr Gratien Griechenlands,
Ihr Himmelstöchter, gegangen,
Daß, wenn die Reise zu weit nicht ist,
Zu uns ihr kommet, ihr Holden!

Wenn milder athmen die Lüfte,
Und liebende Pfeile der Morgen
Uns Allzugedultigen schikt,
Und leichte Gewölke blühn
Uns über den schüchternen Augen,
Dann werden wir sagen, wie kommt
Ihr, Charitinnen, zu Wilden?
Die Dienerinnen des Himmels
Sind aber wunderbar,
Wie alles Göttlichgeborne.
Zum Traume wirds ihm, will es Einer
Beschleichen und straft den, der
Ihm gleichen will mit Gewalt;
Oft überraschet es einen,
Der eben kaum es gedacht hat.

I would not wish to leave her thus
And come merely
To invite you, O Graces of Greece,
Daughters of heaven,
To visit us, O lovely ones,
If the journey be not too far.

When breezes blow more sweetly
And dawn releases loving arrows
In our all too patient midst,
And light clouds blossom
Above our bashful eyes,
We shall ask, How, Charites,
Have you come among barbarians?
But the handmaids of heaven
Are miraculous,
As is everything born of the gods.
Try taking it by surprise, and it turns
To a dream; try matching it by force,
And punishment is the reward;
Often, when you've barely given it
A thought, it just happens.

Der Rhein

An Isaak von Sinclair

Im dunkeln Epheu saß ich, an der Pforte
Des Waldes, eben, da der goldene Mittag,
Den Quell besuchend, herunterkam
Von Treppen des Alpengebirgs,
Das mir die göttlichgebaute,
Die Burg der Himmlischen heißt
Nach alter Meinung, wo aber
Geheim noch manches entschieden
Zu Menschen gelanget; von da
Vernahm ich ohne Vermuthen
Ein Schiksaal, denn noch kaum
War mir im warmen Schatten
Sich manches beredend, die Seele
Italia zu geschweift
Und fernhin an die Küsten Moreas.

Jezt aber, drinn im Gebirg,
Tief unter den silbernen Gipfeln
Und unter fröhlichem Grün,
Wo die Wälder schauernd zu ihm,
Und der Felsen Häupter übereinander
Hinabschaun, taglang, dort
Im kältesten Abgrund hört'
Ich um Erlösung jammern
Den Jüngling, es hörten ihn, wie er tobt',
Und die Mutter Erd' anklagt',
Und den Donnerer, der ihn gezeuget,
Erbarmend die Eltern, doch
Die Sterblichen flohn von dem Ort,
Denn furchtbar war, da lichtlos er
In den Fesseln sich wälzte,
Das Rasen des Halbgotts.

The Rhine

To Isaak von Sinclair

I was sitting in the dark ivy, at the gate
Of the forest, just as the spring was visited
With the gold of noon pouring
Down the steps of the Alps
Which I call the fortress of the gods
In the ancient sense, architected
By the heavens, and from which
Many decrees are still mysteriously
Handed down to men; there,
Against all expectation, I grew aware
Of a fate, even as my soul,
Lost in its own conversation
In the warm shade,
Had already wandered off to Italy
And beyond, to the shores of Morea.

But now, within the mountains,
Deep beneath the silver peaks
And joyous green,
Where shuddering woods
And boulders, head over head,
Look down on him, days
On end, there, in coldest
Abyss, I heard the young man
Moan for deliverance,
Hurling blame at Mother Earth
And his father, the Thunderer,
And his parents felt compassion
For his raving, but mortals fled
The place, terrified by the demigod's
Rage as he wrenched at his chains
In the dark.

Die Stimme wars des edelsten der Ströme,
Des freigeborenen Rheins,
Und anderes hoffte der, als droben von den Brüdern,
Dem Tessin und dem Rhodanus,
Er schied und wandern wollt', und ungeduldig ihn
Nach Asia trieb die königliche Seele.
Doch unverständig ist
Das Wünschen vor dem Schiksaal.
Die Blindesten aber
Sind Göttersöhne. Denn es kennet der Mensch
Sein Haus und dem Thier ward, wo
Es bauen solle, doch jenen ist
Der Fehl, daß sie nicht wissen wohin?
In die unerfahrne Seele gegeben.

Ein Räthsel ist Reinentsprungenes. Auch
Der Gesang kaum darf es enthüllen. Denn
Wie du anfiengst, wirst du bleiben.
So viel auch wirket die Noth,
Und die Zucht, das meiste nemlich
Vermag die Geburt,
Und der Lichtstral, der
Dem Neugebornen begegnet.
Wo aber ist einer,
Um frei zu bleiben
Sein Leben lang, und des Herzens Wunsch
Allein zu erfüllen, so
Aus günstigen Höhn, wie der Rhein,
Und so ans heiligem Schoose
Glüklich geboren, wie jener?

Drum ist ein Jauchzen sein Wort.
Nicht liebt er, wie andere Kinder,
In Wikelbanden zu weinen;
Denn wo die Ufer zuerst
An die Seit ihm schleichen, die krummen,

It was the voice of the noblest of rivers,
The freeborn Rhine,
Whose hopes lay elsewhere when he left
His brothers, Ticino and Rhône, behind,
Bent on adventure, impatiently driven
Towards Asia by his royal soul.
But desire is foolish
In the face of fate.
Yet the blindest
Are sons of gods. For man knows
His house, animals realize
Where to build, but these others
Fail in their inexperience,
They know not where to go.

A riddle, the pure of source. Which
Even song may scarce disclose. For
As you began, so shall you remain,
And though need
And nurture leave their mark,
It all depends on birth,
On the ray of light
The newborn meets.
But where is the man
Who can remain free
His whole life long, alone
Doing his heart's desire,
Like the Rhine, so fortunate
To have been born from
Propitious heights and sacred womb?

His Word is hence a shout of joy.
Unlike other children, he does not
Whimper in swaddling clothes;
For when riverbanks start
Sidling up to him, crooked,

Und durstig umwindend ihn,
Den Unbedachten, zu ziehn
Und wohl zu behüten begehren
Im eigenen Zahne, lachend
Zerreißt er die Schlangen und stürzt
Mit der Beut und wenn in der Eil'
Ein Größerer ihn nicht zähmt,
Ihm wachsen läßt, wie der Bliz, muß er
Die Erde spalten, und wie Bezauberte fliehn
Die Wälder ihm nach und zusammensinkend die Berge.

Ein Gott will aber sparen den Söhnen
Das eilende Leben und lächelt,
Wenn unenthaltsam, aber gehemmt
Von heiligen Alpen, ihm
In der Tiefe, wie jener, zürnen die Ströme.
In solcher Esse wird dann
Auch alles Lautre geschmiedet,
Und schön ists, wie er drauf,
Nachdem er die Berge verlassen,
Stillwandelnd sich im deutschen Lande
Begnüget und das Sehnen stillt
Im guten Geschäffte, wenn er das Land baut
Der Vater Rhein und liebe Kinder nährt
In Städten, die er gegründet.

Doch nimmer, nimmer vergißt ers.
Denn eher muß die Wohnung vergehn,
Und die Sazung und zum Unbild werden
Der Tag der Menschen, ehe vergessen
Ein solcher dürfte den Ursprung
Und die reine Stimme der Jugend.
Wer war es, der zuerst
Die Liebesbande verderbt
Und Strike von ihnen gemacht hat?

Coiled in thirst,
Eager to draw him, unawares,
Into the shelter
Of their teeth, he laughs
And tears these snakes apart,
Plunging onward with the spoils,
And if no higher power tamed his rush,
He would grow and split the earth
Like lightning, as forests hurtled in his wake,
Enchanted, and mountains crashed to the ground.

Yet a god would spare his sons
A life this rash and smiles
When rivers rage at him as this one does
From depths, intemperate,
Though hemmed by holy Alps.
In such forges the unalloyed
Is hammered into shape, and
It is a thing of beauty when he leaves
The mountains, content to flow
Quietly through German lands, his longings
Stilled in fruitful commerce, and
Works the soil, feeding the children
In towns he has founded,
Father Rhine.

But he shall never, never forget.
Human law and habitation would sooner
Perish and the light of man
Be twisted beyond recognition, than
He forget his origin,
The pure voice of his youth.
Who was it who first
Wrecked the bonds of love
And transformed them into chains?

Dann haben des eigenen Rechts
Und gewiß des himmlischen Feuers
Gespottet die Trozigen, dann erst
Die sterblichen Pfade verachtend
Verwegnes erwählt
Und den Göttern gleich zu werden getrachtet.

Es haben aber an eigner
Unsterblichkeit die Götter genug, und bedürfen
Die Himmlischen eines Dings,
So sinds Heroën und Menschen
Und Sterbliche sonst. Denn weil
Die Seeligsten nichts fühlen von selbst,
Muß wohl, wenn solches zu sagen
Erlaubt ist, in der Götter Nahmen
Theilnehmend fühlen ein Andrer,
Den brauchen sie; jedoch ihr Gericht
Ist, daß sein eigenes Haus
Zerbreche der und das Liebste
Wie den Feind schelt' und sich Vater und Kind
Begrabe unter den Trümmern,
Wenn einer, wie sie, seyn will und nicht
Ungleiches dulden, der Schwärmer.

Drum wohl ihm, welcher fand
Ein wohlbeschiedenes Schiksaal,
Wo noch der Wanderungen
Und süß der Leiden Erinnerung
Aufrauscht am sichern Gestade,
Daß da und dorthin gern
Er sehn mag bis an die Grenzen
Die bei der Geburt ihm Gott
Zum Aufenthalte gezeichnet.
Dann ruht er, seeligbescheiden,
Denn alles, was er gewollt,

Which led rebels to make
A mock of their rights
And the heavenly fire and,
Disdaining mortal ways,
Elect presumption,
Striving to become the equals of gods.

But their own immortality
Suffices the gods. If there be
One thing they need
It is heroes and men
And mortals in general. Since
The gods feel nothing
Of themselves, if to speak so
Be permitted, they need
Someone else to share and feel
In their name; yet ordain
That he shall break his own
Home, curse those he loves
Like enemies, and bury father and child
Under rubble, should he seek
To become their equal, fanatic,
Refusing to observe distinctions.

Hence happy is he who has found
A fate to his proportion
Where the memory of trials
And travels whispers sweetly
Against stable shores,
So that his roving eye
Reaches as far as the limits
Of his residence, traced
By God at his birth.
He rests, content with his station,
Now that everything he desired

Das Himmlische, von selber umfängt
Es unbezwungen, lächelnd
Jezt, da er ruhet, den Kühnen.

Halbgötter denk' ich jezt
Und kennen muß ich die Theuern,
Weil oft ihr Leben so
Die sehnende Brust mir beweget.
Wem aber, wie, Rousseau, dir,
Unüberwindlich die Seele
Die starkausdauernde ward,
Und sicherer Sinn
Und süße Gaabe zu hören,
Zu reden so, daß er aus heiliger Fülle
Wie der Weingott, thörig göttlich
Und gesezlos sie die Sprache der Reinesten giebt
Verständlich den Guten, aber mit Recht
Die Achtungslosen mit Blindheit schlägt
Die entweihenden Knechte, wie nenn ich den Fremden?

Die Söhne der Erde sind, wie die Mutter,
Allliebend, so empfangen sie auch
Mühlos, die Glüklichen, Alles.
Drum überraschet es auch
Und schrökt den sterblichen Mann,
Wenn er den Himmel, den
Er mit den liebenden Armen
Sich auf die Schultern gehäufft,
Und die Last der Freude bedenket;
Dann scheint ihm oft das Beste,
Fast ganz vergessen da,
Wo der Stral nicht brennt,
Im Schatten des Walds
Am Bielersee in frischer Grüne zu seyn,
Und sorglosarm an Tönen,
Anfängern gleich, bei Nachtigallen zu lernen.

Of heaven surrounds him
Of its own accord, smiling on him,
Once so headstrong, now at rest.

It's demigods I think of now,
And there must be a way in which
I know them, so often has their life
Stirred my breast with longings.
But a man like you, Rousseau,
Whose soul had the strength to endure
And grow invincible,
Whose sense was sure,
So gifted with powers of hearing
And speaking that, like the winegod,
He overflows and, divine and lawless
In his folly, makes the language of the purest
Accessible to the good, but justly blinds
Those sacrilegious slaves who could not care,
What name should I give this stranger?

The sons of the earth, like their mother,
Love everything, and accept it all
Without effort, lucky ones.
Which is why surprise and fright
Strike mortal man
When he considers the heaven
He has heaped upon his shoulders
With loving arms, and realizes
The burden of joy;
So that it often seems best
To him to remain forgotten
In the shade of the woods,
Away from the burn of light,
Amid the fresh foliage of Lake Bienne,
Caring little how poorly he sings
Schooled, like any beginner, by nightingales.

Und herrlich ists, aus heiligem Schlafe dann
Erstehen und aus Waldes Kühle
Erwachend, Abends nun
Dem milderen Licht entgegenzugehn,
Wenn, der die Berge gebaut
Und den Pfad der Ströme gezeichnet,
Nachdem er lächelnd auch
Der Menschen geschäfftiges Leben
Das othemarme, wie Seegel
Mit seinen Lüften gelenkt hat,
Auch ruht und zu der Schülerin jezt,
Der Bildner, Gutes mehr
Denn Böses findend,
Zur heutigen Erde der Tag sich neiget.—

Dann feiern das Brautfest Menschen und Götter,
Es feiern die Lebenden all,
Und ausgeglichen
Ist eine Weile das Schiksaal.
Und die Flüchtlinge suchen die Heerberg,
Und süßen Schlummer die Tapfern,
Die Liebenden aber
Sind, was sie waren, sie sind
Zu Hauße, wo die Blume sich freuet
Unshädlicher Gluth und die finsteren Bäume
Der Geist umsäuselt, aber die Unversöhnten
Sind umgewandelt und eilen
Die Hände sich ehe zu reichen,
Bevor das freundliche Licht
Hinuntergeht und die Nacht kommt.

Doch einigen eilt
Diß schnell vorüber, andere
Behalten es länger.

And it is glorious to arise
From holy sleep, waking
From the forest cool, and walk
Into the milder evening light,
When He who built the mountains,
And traced the course of streams,
He whose smiling breezes
Filled the busy, luffing life
Of man like sails,
Now rests as well,
And finding more good
Than evil, Day, the sculptor,
Now bends towards
His pupil, the present Earth.

Men and gods then celebrate their marriage,
Every living thing rejoices,
And for a while
Fate achieves a balance.
And fugitives seek asylum,
The brave seek sleep,
But lovers remain
As before, at home
Wherever flowers exult
In harmless fire, and the spirit
Rustles around dim trees, while
The unreconciled are now transformed,
Rushing to take each other's hands
Before the benevolent light
Descends into night.

For some, however, all this
Quickly passes, others
Have a longer hold.

Die ewigen Götter sind
Voll Lebens allzeit; bis in den Tod
Kann aber ein Mensch auch
Im Gedächtniß doch das Beste behalten,
Und dann erlebt er das Höchste.
Nur hat ein jeder sein Maas.
Denn schwer ist zu tragen
Das Unglük, aber schwerer das Glük.
Ein Weiser aber vermocht es
Vom Mittag bis in die Mitternacht,
Und bis der Morgen erglänzte,
Beim Gastmahl helle zu bleiben.

Dir mag auf heißem Pfade unter Tannen oder
Im Dunkel des Eichwalds gehüllt
In Stahl, mein Sinklair! Gott erscheinen oder
In Wolken, du kennst ihn, da du kennest, jugendlich,
Des Guten Kraft, und nimmer ist dir
Verborgen das Lächeln des Herrschers
Bei Tage, wenn
Es fieberhaft und angekettet das
Lebendige scheinet oder auch
Bei Nacht, wenn alles gemischt
Ist ordnungslos und wiederkehrt
Uralte Verwirrung.

The eternal gods are full of life
At all times; but a man
Can also keep the best in mind
Even unto death,
Thus experiencing the Highest.
Yet to each his measure.
For misfortune is heavy
To bear, and fortune weighs yet more.
But a wise man managed to stay lucid
Throughout the banquet,
From noon to midnight,
Until the break of dawn.

Sinclair, my friend, should God appear
To you on a burning path under pines
Or in the dark of oaks, sheathed
In steel, or among clouds, you would
Recognize him, knowing, in your youth,
The power of Good, and the Lord's
Smile never escapes you
By day, when life
Appears fevered and chained,
Or by night, when everything blends
Into confusion, and primeval
Chaos reigns once more.

Der Einzige

Was ist es, das
An die alten seeligen Küsten
Mich fesselt, daß ich mehr noch
Sie liebe, als mein Vaterland?
Denn wie in himmlische
Gefangenschaft verkaufft
Dort bin ich, wo Apollo gieng
In Königsgestalt,
Und zu unschuldigen Jünglingen sich
Herablies Zevs und Söhn' in heiliger Art
Und Töchter zeugte
Der Hohe unter den Menschen?

Der hohen Gedanken
Sind nemlich viel
Entsprungen des Vaters Haupt
Und große Seelen
Von ihm zu Menschen gekommen.
Gehöret hab' ich
Von Elis und Olympia, bin
Gestanden oben auf dem Parnaß,
Und über Bergen des Isthmus,
Und drüben auch
Bei Smyrna und hinab
Bei Ephesos bin ich gegangen;

Viel hab' ich schönes gesehn,
Und gesungen Gottes Bild,
Hab' ich, das lebet unter
Den Menschen, aber dennoch
Ihr alten Götter und all
Ihr tapfern Söhne der Götter
Noch Einen such ich, den

The Only One

What is it that
Binds me to these ancient
Blessed shores, that I love
Them more than my country?
As if sold into
Heavenly bondage,
I am where Apollo
Walked in the guise of a king
And Zeus descended
On innocent youths
And sired sons and daughters
Among mortals by holy means.

Many lofty thoughts
Have sprung from
The Father's brow,
From him great souls
Have come to men.
I have heard
Of Elis and Olympia, have
Stood atop Parnassos
And above the mountains of the Isthmos
And over toward
Smyrna and down
By Ephesos have I walked;

I have seen much beauty
And sung the image of God
Which lives among men,
And yet, O ancient gods
O brave sons of gods,
There is One among you
Whom I love and seek,

Ich liebe unter euch,
Wo ihr den lezten eures Geschlechts
Des Haußes Kleinod mir
Dem fremden Gaste verberget.

Mein Meister und Herr!
O du, mein Lehrer!
Was bist du ferne
Geblieben? und da
Ich fragte unter den Alten,
Die Helden und
Die Götter, warum bliebest
Du aus? Und jezt ist voll
Von Trauern meine Seele
Als eifertet, ihr Himmlischen, selbst
Daß, dien' ich einem, mir
Das andere fehlet.

Ich weiß es aber, eigene Schuld
Ists! Denn zu sehr,
O Christus! häng' ich an dir,
Wiewohl Herakles Bruder
Und kühn bekenn' ich, du
Bist Bruder auch des Eviers, der
An den Wagen spannte
Die Tyger und hinab
Bis an den Indus
Gebietend freudigen Dienst
Den Weinberg stiftet und
Den Grimm bezähmte der Völker.

Es hindert aber eine Schaam
Mich dir zu vergleichen
Die weltlichen Männer. Und freilich weiß
Ich, der dich zeugte, dein Vater,
Derselbe der,

The last of your race,
The jewel of your house
Whom you hide from me,
A passing stranger.

My Master and Lord,
My Teacher,
Why have you kept
So far away? When I
Inquired among the ancients,
Among heroes and
Gods, why did you fail
To appear? And now
My soul is filled with grief,
As if, O gods, you jealously decreed
That serving the one, I
Thereby lose the other.

But I know, the fault
Is all mine. For I cling
Too close to you, Christ,
Though you are Herakles' brother
And, I must confess, the brother
Of Euios too, who
Harnassed tigers to his
Chariot and, commanding
Joyous worship down
To the Indus,
Founded vineyards and
Tamed the wrath of nations.

Yet some sense of shame
Keeps me from comparing
Worldly men to you. And of course
I know who sired you, your Father,
The very one who

Denn nimmer herrscht er allein.

Es hänget aber an Einem
Die Liebe. Diesesmal
Ist nemlich vom eigenen Herzen
Zu sehr gegangen der Gesang,
Gut machen will ich den Fehl
Wenn ich noch andere singe.
Nie treff ich, wie ich wünsche,
Das Maas. Ein Gott weiß aber
Wenn kommet, was ich wünsche das Beste.
Denn wie der Meister
Gewandelt auf Erden
Ein gefangener Aar,

Und viele, die
Ihn sahen, fürchteten sich,
Dieweil sein Äußerstes that
Der Vater und sein Bestes unter
Den Menschen wirkete wirklich,
Und sehr betrübt war auch
Der Sohn so lange, bis er
Gen Himmel fuhr in den Lüften,
Dem gleich ist gefangen die Seele der Helden.
Die Dichter müssen auch
Die geistigen weltlich seyn.

For he never reigns alone.

But love clings
To One. This time
The song has come too deep
From my heart,
Let me mend the error
By singing others.
I never achieve the measure
I wish. But a god knows
When the best I wish comes true.
For like the Master
Who wandered the earth,
A captive eagle,

(And many who saw him
Took fright,
While the Father did
His utmost to realize
His best among men,
And the Son was dark
With grief until he rose
To heaven on the breeze),
Like him, heroes' souls are captive.
Poets, too, men of the spirit,
Must keep to the world.

Patmos

Dem Landgrafen von Homburg

Nah ist
Und schwer zu fassen der Gott.
Wo aber Gefahr ist, wächst
Das Rettende auch.
Im Finstern wohnen
Die Adler und furchtlos gehn
Die Söhne der Alpen über den Abgrund weg
Auf leichtgebaueten Brüken.
Drum, da gehäuft sind rings
Die Gipfel der Zeit, und die Liebsten
Nah wohnen, ermattend auf
Getrenntesten Bergen,
So gieb unschuldig Wasser,
O Fittige gieb uns, treuesten Sinns
Hinüberzugehn und wiederzukehren.

So sprach ich, da entführte
Mich schneller, denn ich vermuthet
Und weit, wohin ich nimmer
Zu kommen gedacht, ein Genius mich
Vom eigenen Hauß'. Es dämmerten
Im Zwielicht, da ich gieng
Der schattige Wald
Und die sehnsüchtigen Bäche
Der Heimath; nimmer kannt' ich die Länder;
Doch bald, in frischem Glanze,
Geheimnißvoll
Im goldenen Rauche, blühte
Schnellaufgewachsen,
Mit Schritten der Sonne,
Mit tausend Gipfeln duftend,

Patmos

To the Landgrave of Homburg

Near and
Hard to grasp, the god.
Yet where danger lies,
Grows that which saves.
Eagles dwell
In darkness, and without fear
The sons of the Alps span the abyss
On lightly built bridges.
Since the peaks of Time lie
Heaped around us and those we love
Live near, languishing
On separate mountains,
Give us innocent waters
O give us wings so that, faithful-minded,
We might cross over and back.

I was saying this, when a genius
Carried me off from my house,
More quickly than expected,
Further than I ever imagined
Going. As I proceeded,
The shady woods
And restless brooks
Of home faded into
Twilight; I no longer recognized the lands below;
But soon thereafter,
Mysterious
In its radiance, surging
From the golden haze
With every stride of the sun
And the fragrance of a thousand peaks,

Mir Asia auf, und geblendet sucht'
Ich eines, das ich kennete, denn ungewohnt
War ich der breiten Gassen, wo herab
Vom Tmolus fährt
Der goldgeschmükte Pactol
Und Taurus stehet und Messogis,
Und voll von Blumen der Garten,
Ein stilles Feuer; aber im Lichte
Blüht hoch der silberne Schnee;
Und Zeug unsterblichen Lebens
An unzugangbaren Wänden
Uralt der Epheu wächst und getragen sind
Von lebenden Säulen, Cedern und Lorbeern
Die feierlichen,
Die göttlichgebauten Palläste.

Es rauschen aber um Asias Thore
Hinziehend da und dort
In ungewisser Meeresebene
Der schattenlosen Straßen genug,
Doch kennt die Inseln der Schiffer.
Und da ich hörte
Der nahegelegenen eine
Sei Patmos,
Verlangte mich sehr,
Dort einzukehren und dort
Der dunkeln Grotte zu nahn.
Denn nicht, wie Cypros,
Die quellenreiche, oder
Der anderen eine
Wohnt herrlich Patmos,

Gastfreundlich aber ist
Im ärmeren Haußе
Sie dennoch
Und wenn vom Schiffbruch oder klagend

Asia burst into flower! Dazzled,
I cast about for a familiar sight,
Unaccustomed to the width of streets
Down which Pactolus all aglitter
Drives from Tmolus,
Where Taurus and Messogis rise
And the garden is ablossom,
A quiet fire. But in the light,
Silver snow blooms on heights
And, proof of immortal life,
Age-old ivy covers
Inaccessible cliffs, while living
Pillars of cedar and laurel support
Triumphant palaces
Built by the gods.

Despite the many waterways
That murmur around the gates of Asia,
Unshaded from the sun, adrift
In the uncertain expanse of sea,
Boatmen know these islands.
And when I heard
That Patmos lay
Among the nearer isles
I was eager
To put ashore and venture
Toward the dark grotto.
For unlike Cypros,
Rich in springs,
Unlike other majestic
Residences,

The house of Patmos
Is poor, yet hospitable,
And should a stranger come
Ashore from shipwreck,

Um die Heimath oder
Den abgeschiedenen Freund
Ihr nahet einer
Der Fremden, hört sie es gern, und ihre Kinder
Die Stimmen des heißen Hains,
Und wo der Sand fällt, und sich spaltet
Des Feldes Fläche, die Laute
Sie hören ihn und liebend tönt
Es wieder von den Klagen des Manns. So pflegte
Sie einst des gottgeliebten,
Des Sehers, der in seeliger Jugend war

Gegangen mit
Dem Sohne des Höchsten, unzertrennlich, denn
Es liebte der Gewittertragende die Einfalt
Des Jüngers und es sahe der achtsame Mann
Das Angesicht des Gottes genau,
Da, beim Geheimnisse des Weinstoks, sie
Zusammensaßen, zu der Stunde des Gastmals,
Und in der großen Seele, ruhigahnend den Tod
Aussprach der Herr und die lezte Liebe, denn nie genug
Hatt' er von Güte zu sagen
Der Worte, damals, und zu erheitern, da
Ers sahe, das Zürnen der Welt.
Denn alles ist gut. Drauf starb er. Vieles wäre
Zu sagen davon. Und es sahn ihn, wie er siegend blikte
Den Freudigsten die Freunde noch zulezt,

Doch trauerten sie, da nun
Es Abend worden, erstaunt,
Denn Großentschiedenes hatten in der Seele
Die Männer, aber sie liebten unter der Sonne
Das Leben und lassen wollten sie nicht
Vom Angesichte des Herrn
Und der Heimath. Eingetrieben war,
Wie Feuer im Eisen, das, und ihnen gieng
Zur Seite der 'Schatte des Lieben.

Lamenting home or some
Lost friend, she is glad
To listen, and her children,
The voices of hot groves,
And the sounds of spilling
Sand and fissures on the face
Of fields, these
All hear him, tenderly
Echoing the man's lament. Thus, long ago,
She cared for the seer, beloved of God,
Who in his blessed youth had

Accompanied
The Almighty's son, never leaving his side, for
The storm-bearer loved the simplicity
Of his disciple, an attentive man
Who clearly saw the face of the god
As they sat together at the banquet hour
In the mystery of the vine;
And, calm foreboding within his great soul, the Lord
Pronounced his own death and ultimate love,
Unable to find words enough for kindness,
Nor words to cheer his sight
Of the raging world.
For All is Good. Whereupon he died. Much could be
Said of this. And his friends witnessed
His triumphant glance to the very end,

Yet they mourned, now that
Evening had come, astounded
At the great decisive thing that swept
Their souls, but since they loved life
Under the sun, they would not relinquish
The face of the Lord
Or their home. This was driven into them
As fire into iron, and the one they loved
Walked by their side, a shadow.

Drum sandt' er ihnen
Den Geist, und freilich bebte
Das Haus und die Wetter Gottes rollten
Ferndonnernd über
Die ahnenden Häupter, da, schwersinnend
Versammelt waren die Todeshelden,

Izt, da er scheidend
Noch einmal ihnen erschien.
Denn izt erlosch der Sonne Tag
Der Königliche und zerbrach
Den geradestralenden,
Den Zepter, göttlichleidend, von selbst,
Denn wiederkommen sollt es
Zu rechter Zeit. Nicht wär es gut
Gewesen, später, und schroffabbrechend, untreu,
Der Menschen Werk, und Freude war es
Von nun an,
Zu wohnen in liebender Nacht, und bewahren
In einfältigen Augen, unverwandt
Abgründe der Weisheit. Und es grünen
Tief an den Bergen auch lebendige Bilder,

Doch furchtbar ist, wie da und dort
Unendlich hin zerstreut das Lebende Gott.
Den schon das Angesicht
Der theuern Freunde zu lassen
Und fernhin über die Berge zu gehn
Allein, wo zweifach
Erkannt, einstimmig
War himmlischer Geist; und nicht geweissagt war es, sondern
Die Loken ergriff es, gegenwärtig,
Wenn ihnen plözlich
Ferneilend zurük blikte
Der Gott und schwörend,

For this reason he sent them
The Spirit, and their house was filled
With trembling, and the storms of the Lord
Thundered far above
Their expectant heads, as they sat together
In perplexity, these heroes of death,

Now that he appeared to them
Once again in farewell.
And now the kingly sun's
Light went out and broke
His sceptered beams
In godly pain, due
To return when times
Were right. Far worse, had it
Happened later, brutally tearing men
From their work, so from now on
It was a joy
To live in loving night, to keep
Abysses of wisdom
Fixed in clear eyes. And living images
Grow green in the depths of mountains

Though it is fearsome how God
Scatters Life in all directions.
And fearsome to leave the face
Of one's dear friends and travel
Far over the mountains
Where the heavenly Spirit
Was twice
Perceived, in unanimity; nor had this been prophesied,
Instead a presence seized them by the hair, as
The god, hastening away, suddenly
Shot them back a glance,
And imploring him to stay,

Damit er halte, wie an Seilen golden
Gebunden hinfort
Das Böse nennend, sie die Hände sich reichten—

Wenn aber stirbt alsdenn
An dem am meisten
Die Schönheit hieng, daß an der Gestalt
Ein Wunder war und die Himmlischen gedeutet
Auf ihn, und wenn, ein Räthsel ewig füreinander
Sie sich nicht fassen können
Einander, die zusammenlebten
Im Gedächtniß, und nicht den Sand nur oder
Die Weiden es hinwegnimmt und die Tempel
Ergreifft, wenn die Ehre
Des Halbgotts und der Seinen
Verweht und selber sein Angesicht
Der Höchste wendet
Darob, daß nirgend ein
Unsterbliches mehr am Himmel zu sehn ist oder
Auf grüner Erde, was ist diß?

Es ist der Wurf des Säemanns, wenn er faßt
Mit der Schaufel den Waizen,
Und wirft, dem Klaren zu, ihn schwingend über die Tenne.
Ihm fällt die Schaale vor den Füßen, aber
Ans Ende kommet das Korn,
Und nicht ein Übel ists, wenn einiges
Verloren gehet und von der Rede
Verhallet der lebendige Laut,
Denn göttliches Werk auch gleichet dem unsern,
Nicht alles will der Höchste zumal.
Zwar Eisen träget der Schacht,
Und glühende Harze der Aetna,
So hätt' ich Reichtum,
Ein Bild zu bilden, und ähnlich
Zu schaun, wie er gewesen, den Christ,

Calling Evil by its name,
Now bound as by golden ropes,
They reached out their hands—

But when he dies,
To whom beauty
So adhered that his person
Was a miracle, designated
By the gods, and when they forever become
Enigmas to each other, and elude each
Other's grasp, they who lived in common
Memory of him, and when sand
And willows are blown away, and temples
Are destroyed, when the honor
Of the demigod and his disciples
Is scattered to the winds and even
The Almighty averts
His face, leaving nothing
Immortal to be seen in the sky
Or on green earth, what is this?

It is the winnower scooping wheat
In his shovel and swinging it
Into the clear above the threshing floor.
The chaff falls at his feet, but
In the end the grain lies sifted,
No harm if some of it
Be lost or the living echo
Of his Word grow faint,
For the work of gods resembles ours;
The Almighty does not wish all things at once.
Just as mines yield ore
And Etna glows with resins,
I would have enough in my possession
To shape an image of him and
Contemplate Christ as he was,

Wenn aber einer spornte sich selbst,
Und traurig redend, unterweges, da ich wehrlos wäre
Mich überfiele, daß ich staunt' und von dem Gotte
Das Bild nachahmen möcht' ein Knecht—
Im Zorne sichtbar sah' ich einmal
Des Himmels Herrn, nicht, daß ich seyn sollt etwas, sondern
Zu lernen. Gütig sind sie, ihr Verhaßtestes aber ist,
So lange sie herrschen, das Falsche, und es gilt
Dann Menschliches unter Menschen nicht mehr.
Denn sie nicht walten, es waltet aber
Unsterblicher Schiksaal und es wandelt ihr Werk
Von selbst, und eilend geht es zu Ende.
Wenn nemlich höher gehet himmlischer
Triumphgang, wird genennet, der Sonne gleich
Von Starken der frohlokende Sohn des Höchsten,

Ein Loosungszeichen, und hier ist der Stab
Des Gesanges, niederwinkend,
Denn nichts ist gemein. Die Todten weket
Er auf, die noch gefangen nicht
Vom Rohen sind. Es warten aber
Der scheuen Augen viele
Zu schauen das Licht. Nicht wollen
Am scharfen Strale sie blühn,
Wiewohl den Muth der goldene Zaum hält.
Wenn aber, als
Von schwellenden Augenbraunen
Der Welt vergessen
Stillleuchtende Kraft aus heiliger Schrift fällt, mögen
Der Gnade sich freuend, sie
Am stillen Blike sich üben.

But if someone were spurred to set upon me
With sorry words as I made my way
Defenseless and amazed, as if a slave
Could imitate the image of God—
I once saw the lords of heaven
Visibly furious that I wanted to *be* something
Rather than learn. They are benevolent
But brook no falsity as long as they reign,
Lest man forget what is human.
For man does not govern, the power lies
With Fate, and the work of the immortals moves
Of its own pace, hasting towards completion.
When heaven's triumphal march reaches
Its height, strong men shall give the Almighty's
Jubilant son a name much like the sun,

A sign of deliverance, and here is the staff
Of song, beckoning down to us,
For nothing is too lowly. He wakes
The dead who are not yet captives
Of cruder forces. Yet many timid
Eyes await a glimpse
Of the light, reluctant
To flower in the glare,
Their courage bridled by the gold.
But when the quiet radiant force of holy scripture falls
As from the threshold of brows
Oblivious to the world,
They can exercise
Their silent gaze,
Rejoicing in grace.

Und wenn die Himmlischen jezt
So, wie ich glaube, mich lieben
Wie viel mehr Dich,
Denn Eines weiß ich,
Daß nemlich der Wille
Des ewigen Vaters viel
Dir gilt. Still ist sein Zeichen
Am donnernden Himmel. Und Einer stehet darunter
Sein Leben lang. Denn noch lebt Christus.
Es sind aber die Helden, seine Söhne
Gekommen all und heilige Schriften
Von ihm und den Bliz erklären
Die Thaten der Erde bis izt,
Ein Wettlauf unaufhaltsam. Er ist aber dabei. Denn seine Werke
    sind
Ihm alle bewußt von jeher.

Zu lang, zu lang schon ist
Die Ehre der Himmlischen unsichtbar.
Denn fast die Finger müssen sie
Uns führen und schmählich
Entreißt das Herz uns eine Gewalt.
Denn Opfer will der Himmlischen jedes,
Wenn aber eines versäumt ward,
Nie hat es Gutes gebracht.
Wir haben gedienet der Mutter Erd'
Und haben jüngst dem Sonnenlichte gedient,
Unwissend, der Vater aber liebt,
Der über allen waltet,
Am meisten, daß gepfleget werde
Der veste Buchstab, und bestehendes gut
Gedeutet. Dem folgt deutscher Gesang.

And if, as I believe,
The gods now love me,
How much more must they love you.
For this I know,
The will of the eternal Father
Means much to you. His sign
Is silent in the thundering sky.
Under which a sole figure stands
His whole life long. Christ lives.
But the heroes, his other sons, have all
Appeared, and holy scriptures
Concerning him, and in their endless race
To the present, the events of the world
Elucidate the lightning. But in this he takes part. His
　　　　works
Have all been known to him from the very start.

Ah, the glory of the gods
Has lain invisible far too long.
They almost have to guide
Our fingers and, shamefully, only by force
Do we give up our hearts.
For each god requires sacrifice,
Nothing good has ever come
From neglect.
We have served our Mother Earth
And served the sunlight lately,
Unawares, but what our Father
Who reigns supreme
Most loves is that we keep the letter
Fast in our care and well interpret
What endures. Which German song obeys.

Patmos

Bruchstücke der späteren Fassung

Vom Jordan und von Nazareth
Und fern vom See, an Capernaum,
Und Galiläa die Lüfte, und von Cana.
Eine Weile bleib ich, sprach er. Also mit Tropfen
Stillt er das Seufzen des Lichts, das durstigem Wild
War ähnlich in den Tagen, als um Syrien
Jammert der getödteten Kindlein heimatliche
Anmuth im Sterben, und das Haupt
Des Täuffers gepflükt, war unverwelklicher Schrift gleich
Sichtbar auf weilender Schüssel. Wie Feuer
Sind Stimmen Gottes. Schwer ists aber
Im Großen zu behalten das Große.
Nicht eine Waide. Daß einer
Bleibet im Anfang. Jezt aber
Geht dieses wieder, wie sonst.

Johannes. Christus. Diesen möcht'
Ich singen, gleich dem Herkules, oder
Der Insel, welche vestgehalten und gerettet, erfrischend
Die benachbarte mit kühlen Meereswassern aus der Wüste
Der Fluth, der weiten, Peleus. Das geht aber
Nicht. Anders ists ein Schiksaal. Wundervoller.
Reicher, zu singen. Unabsehlich
Seit jenem die Fabel. Und jezt
Möcht' ich die Fahrt der Edelleute nach
Jerusalem, und das Leiden irrend in Canossa,
Und den Heinrich singen. Daß aber
Der Muth nicht selber mich aussezze. Begreiffen müssen
Diß wir zuvor. Wie Morgenluft sind nemlich die Nahmen
Seit Christus. Werden Träume. Fallen, wie Irrtum
Auf das Herz und tödtend, wenn nicht einer

Patmos

[Fragments of a later version]

From Jordan and from Nazareth
And far off from the sea, toward Capernaum
And from Galilee, the breezes, and from Canaan.
I shall tarry a while, said he. Then drop by drop
He stilled the sighing of the light, which was like
Wild beasts thirsting in the days when the wail
Of murdered infants went through Syria, as they died
With native grace, and the head
Of the Baptist lay plucked upon the platter, visible
As a script that will not wilt. The voices of God
Are as fire. Yet with events this great
It is hard to keep the main thing straight.
This is no pasture. One must
Stick to the beginning. But now
Things are starting over as before.

John. Christ. Let me sing
Of the latter as of Hercules or
The island, bounded by cool ocean waters,
Which held and rescued Peleus, refreshment
After the wide desert of waves. But this
Doesn't work. A fate rings differently. More wonderful.
Richer to sing. The myth is
Unfathomable ever since Him. And now
Let me sing the journey of the knights
To Jerusalem, and Heinrich wandering
In pain at Canossa. Let
My courage not abandon me. But first,
We must grasp this. Names are as the morning breeze
Ever since Christ. Become dreams. Fall, like error,
Upon the heart, and can kill if you do not

Erwäget, was sie sind und begreift.
Es sah aber der achtsame Mann
Das Angesicht des Gottes,
Damals, da, beim Geheimnisse des Weinstoks sie
Zusammensaßen, zu der Stunde des Gastmals,
Und in der großen Seele, wohlauswählend, den Tod
Aussprach der Herr, und die lezte Liebe, denn nie genug
Hatt er, von Güte, zu sagen
Der Worte, damals, und zu bejahn bejahendes. Aber sein Licht
    war
Tod. Denn karg ist das Zürnen der Welt.
Das aber erkannt' er. Alles ist gut. Drauf starb er.
Es sahen aber, gebükt, deß ungeachtet, vor Gott die Gestalt
Des Verläugnenden, wie wenn
Ein Jahrhundert sich biegt, nachdenklich, in der Freude der
    Wahrheit
Noch zulezt die Freunde,

Doch trauerten sie, da nun
Es Abend worden. Nemlich rein
Zu seyn, ist Geschik, ein Leben, das ein Herz hat,
Vor solchem Angesicht', und dauert über die Hälfte.
Zu meiden aber ist viel. Zu viel aber
Der Liebe, wo Anbetung ist,
Ist gefahrreich, triffet am meisten. Jene wollten aber
Vom Angesichte des Herrn
Nicht lassen und der Heimath. Eingeboren
Wie Feuer war in dem Eisen das, und ihnen
Zur Seite gieng, wie eine Seuche, der Schatte des Lieben.
Drum sandt er ihnen
Den Geist, und freilich bebte
Das Haus und die Wetter Gottes rollten
Ferndonnernd, Männer schaffend, wie wenn Drachenzähne,
                prächtigen Schiksaals,

Weigh what they are, and understand.
But the attentive man
Saw the face of the god
As they sat together at the banquet hour
In the mystery of the vine,
And having well decided in his great soul, the Lord
Pronounced his own death and ultimate love,
Unable to find words enough for kindness
Or enough yeses for affirmation. But his light was
Death. For the world's wrath is terse.
This he recognized. All is Good. Whereupon he died.
But his friends saw the figure of the Renouncer
To the very end, as they bent
Before God, like a century pensively
Bowed with the joy of truth,

Yet they mourned now that
Evening had come. To remain pure
In the face of such is destiny, is a life
With a heart that will outlive its half.
Yet there is much to be avoided. Excess
Of love in adoration
Is perilous, strikes most often. But these men
Would not relinquish the face
Of the Lord or their home. This was inborn
In them as fire in iron, and the shadow
Of the one they loved walked by their side, a plague.
For this reason he sent them
The Spirit, and their house was filled
With trembling, and the storms of the Lord
Thundered in the distance, creating men, as when dragon's teeth,
                                        of a glorious fate,

Andenken

Der Nordost wehet,
Der liebste unter den Winden
Mir, weil er feurigen Geist
Und gute Fahrt verheißet den Schiffern.
Geh aber nun und grüße
Die schöne Garonne,
Und die Gärten von Bourdeaux
Dort, wo am scharfen Ufer
Hingehet der Steg und in den Strom
Tief fällt der Bach, darüber aber
Hinschauet ein edel Paar
Von Eichen und Silberpappeln;

Noch denket das mir wohl und wie
Die breiten Gipfel neiget
Der Ulmwald, über die Mühl',
Im Hofe aber wächset ein Feigenbaum.
An Feiertagen gehn
Die braunen Frauen daselbst
Auf seidnen Boden,
Zur Märzenzeit,
Wenn gleich ist Nacht und Tag,
Und über langsamen Stegen,
Von goldenen Träumen schwer,
Einwiegende Lüfte ziehen.

Es reiche aber,
Des dunkeln Lichtes voll,
Mir einer den duftenden Becher,
Damit ich ruhen möge; denn süß
Wär' unter Schatten der Schlummer.
Nicht ist es gut,
Seellos von sterblichen

Remembrance

The northeasterly blows in,
My favorite among winds,
Since it promises fire
And safe passage to sailors.
But go now and greet
The lovely Garonne
And the gardens of Bordeaux,
There, where the path cuts
Along the shore and the stream dives
Riverward, but a noble pair
Of oaks and white poplars
Looks on from above;

All this still comes to mind and how
The broad tops of elms
Bend over the mill,
But a figtree is growing in the courtyard.
There, on feastdays,
Brown women walk
The silky ground,
Toward March,
When night and day are equal,
And down leisurely paths
Heavy with golden dreams,
Drift lulling breezes.

But someone reach me
A fragrant cupful
Of dark light, that
I might rest; it would be sweet
To drowse in the shade.
It is no good
To let mortal thoughts

Gedanken zu seyn. Doch gut
Ist ein Gespräch und zu sagen
Des Herzens Meinung, zu hören viel
Von Tagen der Lieb',
Und Thaten, welche geschehen.

Wo aber sind die Freunde? Bellarmin
Mit dem Gefährten? Mancher
Trägt Scheue, an die Quelle zu gehn;
Es beginnet nemlich der Reichtum
Im Meere. Sie,
Wie Mahler, bringen zusammen
Das Schöne der Erd' und verschmähn
Den geflügelten Krieg nicht, und
Zu wohnen einsam, jahrlang, unter
Dem entlaubten Mast, wo nicht die Nacht durchglänzen
Die Feiertage der Stadt,
Und Saitenspiel und eingeborener Tanz nicht.

Nun aber sind zu Indiern
Die Männer gegangen,
Dort an der luftigen Spiz'
An Traubenbergen, wo herab
Die Dordogne kommt,
Und zusammen mit der prächt'gen
Garonne meerbreit
Ausgehet der Strom. Es nehmet aber
Und giebt Gedächtniß die See,
Und die Lieb' auch heftet fleißig die Augen,
Was bleibet aber, stiften die Dichter.

Rob you of your soul. Yet
Dialogue is good and to speak
The heart, to hear all
About the days of love
And deeds that have taken place.

But where are my friends? Bellarmin
With his companion? There are those
Who shy from the source;
Since riches begin
At sea. Like
Painters, they gather
The beauty of the earth, nor refuse
Wings of war or years lived
Alone beneath a mast
Without leaves, where the night is not
Brightened by the feastdays of the city,
Nor by lyre or native dances.

But now the men are gone
To the Indies,
From that breezy spit of land
And hillsides of grapes, where
The Dordogne descends
Toward the majestic Garonne
And the two flow out
As one wide sea. But memory
Is taken and given by the ocean,
And the eyes of love do not waver in their gaze,
But poets establish what remains.

Der Ister

Jezt komme, Feuer!
Begierig sind wir
Zu schauen den Tag,
Und wenn die Prüfung
Ist durch die Knie gegangen,
Mag einer spüren das Waldgeschrei.
Wir singen aber vom Indus her
Fernangekommen und
Vom Alpheus, lange haben
Das Schikliche wir gesucht,
Nicht ohne Schwingen mag
Zum Nächsten einer greifen
Geradezu
Und kommen auf die andere Seite.
Hier aber wollen wir bauen.
Denn Ströme machen urbar
Das Land. Wenn nemlich Kräuter wachsen
Und an denselben gehn
Im Sommer zu trinken die Thiere,
So gehn auch Menschen daran.

Man nennet aber diesen den Ister.
Schön wohnt er. Es brennet der Säulen Laub,
Und reget sich. Wild stehn
Sie aufgerichtet, untereinander; darob
Ein zweites Maas, springt vor
Von Felsen das Dach. So wundert
Mich nicht, daß er
Den Herkules zu Gaste geladen,
Fernglänzend, am Olympos drunten,
Da der, sich Schatten zu suchen
Vom heißen Isthmos kam,

The Ister

Come to us, fire!
We are avid
For sight of day,
And when the ordeal
Has passed through the knees,
Woodsong is within hearing.
But we sing, having come
Far from the Indus
And Alpheus, we have long sought
Adequacy to fate,
It takes wings to seize
The nearest things
Immediately
And reach the other side.
Let us settle here.
For the rivers make the land
Arable. If there be vegetation
And animals come to water
At the banks in summer,
Here men will also go.

And they call this the Ister.
Beautiful his dwelling. Leaves on columns
Burn and quiver. They stand in the wild,
Rising among each other; above which
Surges a second mass,
The roofing of rock. So it does not
Surprise me he had
Hercules as a guest,
Far-shining, up from Olympos,
Having left the Isthmos heat
In search of shade,

Denn voll des Muthes waren
Daselbst sie, es bedarf aber, der Geister wegen,
Der Kühlung auch. Darum zog jener lieber
An die Wasserquellen hieher und gelben Ufer,
Hoch duftend oben, und schwarz
Vom Fichtenwald, wo in den Tiefen
Ein Jäger gern lustwandelt
Mittags, und Wachstum hörbar ist
An harzigen Bäumen des Isters,

Der scheinet aber fast
Rükwärts zu gehen und
Ich mein, er müsse kommen
Von Osten.
Vieles wäre
Zu sagen davon. Und warum hängt er
An den Bergen gerad? Der andre
Der Rhein ist seitwärts
Hinweggegangen. Umsonst nicht gehn
Im Troknen die Ströme. Aber wie? Ein Zeichen braucht es
Nichts anderes, schlecht und recht, damit es Sonn
Und Mond trag' im Gemüth', untrennbar,
Und fortgeh, Tag und Nacht auch, und
Die Himmlischen warm sich fühlen aneinander.
Darum sind jene auch
Die Freude des Höchsten. Denn wie käm er
Herunter? Und wie Hertha grün,
Sind sie die Kinder des Himmels. Aber Allzugedultig
Scheint der mir, nicht
Freier, und fast zu spotten. Nemlich wenn

For though they had great fortitude
In that place, spirits also need
The cool. He therefore chose
To travel to these springs and yellow banks
With their ascending fragrance and black
With firs, and these valleys
That hunters love to roam
At noon, when you can hear the growing
Of the resinous trees of the Ister

Which almost seems
To run backwards and
Strikes me must come
From the East.
Much could be said
Of this. And why does he cling
So steep to these hills? The other,
The Rhine, ran off
Sideways. There is a reason rivers run
Through dry land. But how? All that is needed
Is a sign, pure and simple, which bears
Sun and moon in mind, indivisible,
And goes its way night and day, and
The gods will feel each other's warmth.
Which is why rivers
Are the Almighty's joy. How could He otherwise
Descend? And like green Hertha,
They are the children of heaven. Yet this one here
Strikes me as all too placid, barely
Free, almost laughable. For when

Angehen soll der Tag
In der Jugend, wo er zu wachsen
Anfängt, es treibet ein anderer da
Hoch schon die Pracht, und Füllen gleich
In den Zaum knirscht er, und weithin hören
Das Treiben die Lüfte,
Ist der zufrieden;
Es brauchet aber Stiche der Fels
Und Furchen die Erd',
Unwirthbar wär es, ohne Weile;
Was aber jener thuet der Strom,
Weis niemand.

In his youth
The day comes for him to begin
To grow, the Rhine is already there,
Driving his splendor higher, champing at the bit
Like a colt, with the winds hearing
His passage in the distance,
While this one lies content.
But rock needs splitting,
Earth needs furrowing,
No habitation unless one linger;
But what he does, the river,
Nobody knows.

Mnemosyne

Ein Zeichen sind wir, deutungslos
Schmerzlos sind wir und haben fast
Die Sprache in der Fremde verloren.
Wenn nemlich über Menschen
Ein Streit ist an dem Himmel und gewaltig
Die Monde gehn, so redet
Das Meer und Ströme müssen
Den Pfad sich suchen. Zweifellos
Ist aber Einer, der
Kann täglich es ändern. Kaum bedarf er
Gesez. Und es tönet das Blatt und Eichbäume wehn dann neben
Den Firnen. Denn nicht vermögen
Die Himmlischen alles. Nemlich es reichen
Die Sterblichen eh' an den Abgrund. Also wendet es sich, das
        Echo
Mit diesen. Lang ist
Die Zeit, es ereignet sich aber
Das Wahre.

Wie aber liebes? Sonnenschein
Am Boden sehen wir und trokenen Staub
Und tief mit Schatten die Wälder und es blühet
An Dächern der Rauch, bei alter Krone
Der Thürme, friedsam; gut sind nemlich,
Hat gegenredend die Seele
Ein Himmlisches verwundet, die Tageszeichen.
Denn Schnee, wie Majenblumen
Das Edelmüthige, wo
Es seie, bedeutend, glänzet auf der grünen Wiese
Der Alpen, hälftig
Da, vom Kreuze redend, das
Gesezt ist unterwegs einmal
Gestorbenen, auf hoher Straß'
Ein Wandersmann geht zornig,

Mnemosyne

A sign we are, without meaning
Without pain we are and have nearly
Lost our language in foreign lands,
For when the heavens quarrel
Over humans and moons proceed
In force, the sea
Speaks out and rivers must find
Their way. But there is One,
Without doubt, who
Can change this any day. He needs
No law. The rustle of leaf and then the sway of oaks
Beside glaciers. Not everything
Is in the power of the gods. Mortals would sooner
Reach toward the abyss. With them
The echo turns. Though the time
Be long, truth
Will come to pass.

But what we love? We see sunshine
On the floor and motes of dust
And the shadows of our native woods and smoke
Blooms from rooftops, at peace beside
Turrets' ancient crowns; for the signs
Of day are good if a god have scarred
The soul in response.
Snow, like lilies of the valley,
Signifying a site
Of nobility, half gleams
With the green of the Alpine meadow
Where, talking of a wayside cross
Commemorating the dead,
A traveler climbs in a rage,

Fernahnend mit
Dem andern, aber was ist diß?

Am Feigenbaum ist mein
Achilles mir gestorben,
Und Ajax liegt
An den Grotten der See,
An Bächen, benachbart dem Skamandros.
An Schläfen Sausen ist, nach
Der unbewegten Salamis steter
Gewohnheit, in der Fremd' ist groß
Ajax gestorben.
Patroklos aber in des Königes Harnisch. Und es starben
Noch andere viel. Am Kithäron aber lag
Elevtherä, der Mnemosyne Stadt. Der auch, als
Ablegte den Mantel Gott, das abendliche nachher löste
Die Loken. Himmlische nemlich sind
Unwillig, wenn einer nicht
Die Seele schonend sich
Zusammengenommen, aber er muß doch; dem
Gleich fehlet die Trauer.

Sharing distant premonitions with
The other, but what is this?

By the figtree
My Achilles died,
And Ajax lies
By the grottoes of the sea,
By streams, with Skamandros as neighbor.
In the persisting tradition of Salamis,
Great Ajax died
Of the roar in his temples
And on foreign soil, unlike
Patroklos, dead in king's armor. And many
Others also died. On Kithairon
Lay Eleutherai, city of Mnemosyne. And when
God cast off his cloak, the darkness came to cut
Her lock of hair. For the gods grow
Indignant if a man
Not gather himself to save
His soul, yet he has no choice; like-
Wise, mourning is in error.

Drafts of Hymns

[Wie Vögel langsam ziehn . . .]

Wie Vögel langsam ziehn
Es bliket voraus
Der Fürst und kühl wehn
An die Brust ihm die Begegnisse wenn
Es um ihn schweiget, hoch
In der Luft, reich glänzend aber hinab
Das Gut ihm liegt der Länder, und mit ihm sind
Das erstemal siegforschend die Jungen.
Er aber mäßiget mit
Der Fittige Schlag.

[As birds drift by . . .]

As birds drift by,
He casts his gaze ahead,
The Prince, each encounter
A cool breeze on his breast, when
Silence falls about him, high
In the air, but bright beneath him
Lie his rich estates, and by his side
The young, eager for their first spoils.
But his wingbeat
Gives them measure.

[Wie Meeresküsten . . .]

Wie Meeresküsten, wenn zu baun
Anfangen die Himmlischen und herein
Schifft unaufhaltsam, eine Pracht, das Werk
Der Woogen, eins ums andere, und die Erde
Sich rüstet aus, darauf vom Freudigsten eines
Mit guter Stimmung, zu recht es legend also schlägt es
Dem Gesang, mit dem Weingott, vielverheißend dem
    bedeutenden
Und der Lieblingin
Des Griechenlandes
Der meergeborenen, schiklich blikenden
Das gewaltige Gut and Ufer.

[Like seacoasts . . .]

Like seacoasts, when the gods
Begin to build, and splendor
Upon splendor comes sailing in, work
Of many a wave, and the earth,
In full array, recieves an envoy of the Lord of Joy
Who sets it all in tune, so song
Is struck by the winegod, prophetic,
And by the darling
Of Greece,
The sea-sired, fair-sighted girl,
Treasure cast on shore.

Heimath

Und niemand weiß

Indessen laß mich wandeln
Und wilde Beeren pflüken
Zu löschen die Liebe zu dir
An deinen Pfaden, o Erd'

Hier wo
        und Rosendornen
Und süße Linden duften neben
Den Buchen, des Mittags, wenn im falben Kornfeld
Das Wachstum rauscht, an geradem Halm,
Und den Naken die Ähre seitwärts beugt
Dem Herbste gleich, jezt aber unter hohem
Gewölbe der Eichen, da ich sinn
Und aufwärts frage, der Glokenschlag
Mir wohlbekannt
Fernher tönt, goldenklingend, um die Stunde, wenn
Der Vogel wieder wacht. So gehet es wohl.

Home

And no one knows

Meanwhile let me roam
And pick wild berries
To quiet my love for you
Upon your paths, O Earth

Here where
                     and the thorns of roses
And sweet lindens cast their fragrance
Beside the beeches, at noon, when the pale rye
Rustles with the growth of slender stalks,
Their ears bowed to the side
Like autumn, but beneath the high
Vault of oaks, as I muse
And question the sky, the sound of bells
I know well
From afar rings golden at the hour
Of reawakening birds. So it goes.

[Wenn nemlich der Rebe Saft . . .]

Wenn nemlich der Rebe Saft,
Das milde Gewächs suchet Schatten
Und die Traube wächset unter dem kühlen
Gewölbe der Blätter,
Den Männern eine Stärke,
Wohl aber duftend den Jungfraun,
Und Bienen,
Wenn sie, vom Wohlgeruche
Des Frühlings trunken, der Geist
Der Sonne rühret, irren ihr nach
Die Getriebenen, wenn aber
Ein Stral brennt, kehren sie
Mit Gesumm, vielahnend
     darob
Die Eiche rauschet,

[When the sap . . .]

When the sap of the vine,
This gentle plant, seeks out shade
And the grape grows beneath the cool
Vault of leaves,
A source of strength to men
But fragrant to young girls
And bees
When, drunk on the scent
Of Spring, they are stirred
By the spirit of the sun, driven
Erratic in its pursuit, but when
Burnt by a ray, they all veer back
Abuzz, filled with premonition
        above
    The oak tree rustles,

[Auf falbem Laube . . .]

Auf falbem Laube ruhet
Die Traube, des Weines Hoffnung, also ruhet auf der Wange
Der Schatten von dem goldenen Schmuk, der hängt
Am Ohre der Jungfrau.

Und ledig soll ich bleiben
Leicht fanget aber sich
In der Kette, die
Es abgerissen, das Kälblein.

Fleißig

Es liebet aber der Sämann
Zu sehen eine,
Des Tages schlafend über
Dem Strikstrumpf.

Nicht will wohllauten
Der deutsche Mund
Aber lieblich
Am stechenden Bart rauschen
Die Küsse.

[On pale leaf . . .]

On pale leaf rests
The grape, this hope of wine, as on the cheek
Rests the shadow of the gold that hangs
From the young girl's ear.

And I must stay single,
Yet the calf ends up
Tangled in the tether
It breaks.

Diligent

Yet the sower
Likes seeing a woman
Asleep over her knitting
During the day.

The German tongue
Will not please the ear
But kisses
Rasp sweetly
On prickly beard.

An die Madonna

Viel hab' ich dein
Und deines Sohnes wegen
Gelitten, o Madonna,
Seit ich gehöret von ihm
In süßer Jugend;
Denn nicht der Seher allein,
Es stehen unter einem Schiksaal
Die Dienenden auch. Denn weil ich

Und manchen Gesang, den ich
Dem höchsten zu singen, dem Vater
Gesonnen war, den hat
Mir weggezehret die Schwermuth.

Doch Himmlische, doch will ich
Dich feiern und nicht soll einer
Der Rede Schönheit mir
Die heimatliche, vorwerfen,
Dieweil ich allein
Zum Felde gehe, wo wild
Die Lilie wächst, furchtlos,
Zum unzugänglichen,
Uralten Gewölbe
Des Waldes,
        das Abendland,

            und gewaltet über
Den Menschen hat, statt anderer Gottheit sie
Die allvergessende Liebe.

Denn damals sollt es beginnen
Als

To the Madonna

For your sake
And your son's, O Madonna,
I have suffered much
Since I first heard of him
In my tender youth;
For the seer is not alone
But stands under a fate
Common to those who serve. Because I

And the many songs I had
In mind to sing to the Father
Most High, these
Sadness stole from me.

Yet, heavenly one, I will
Sing your praise, and let no one
Reproach the beauty
Of my homegrown speech
As I go to the fields
Alone, where the lily
Grows wild, without fear,
And into the impenetrable
Primeval vault
Of the forest,
            the Occident,

                        and she has had power
Over men, in place of the other gods, this
All-forgetting Love.

For it was to have begun
When

Geboren dir im Schoose
Der göttliche Knabe und um ihn
Der Freundin Sohn, Johannes genannt
Vom stummen Vater, der kühne
Dem war gegeben
Der Zunge Gewalt,
Zu deuten

Und die Furcht der Völker und
Die Donner und
Die stürzenden Wasser des Hern.

Denn gut sind Sazungen, aber
Wie Drachenzähne, schneiden sie
Und tödten das Leben, wenn im Zorne sie schärft
Ein Geringer oder ein König.
Gleichmuth ist aber gegeben
Den Liebsten Gottes. So dann starben jene.
Die Beiden,   so auch sahst
Du göttlichtrauernd in der starken Seele sie sterben.
Und wohnst deswegen

                              und wenn in heiliger Nacht
Der Zukunft einer gedenkt und Sorge für
Die sorglosschlafenden trägt
Die frischaufblühenden Kinder
Kömmst lächelnd du, und fragst, was er, wo du
Die Königin seiest, befürchte.

Denn nimmer vermagst du es
Die keimenden Tage zu neiden,
Denn lieb ist dirs, von je,
Wenn größer die Söhne sind,
Denn ihre Mutter. Und nimmer gefällt es dir
Wenn rükwärtsblikend

Born from your womb
The godly child whom
Your kinswoman's son—named John
By his mute father, the keen one—
Was given the power
Of tongue
To interpret

And the nations in terror
The thunders and
The rushing waters of the Lord.

For laws are good, but
Like dragon's teeth they cut
And kill life when whetted
By common or kingly rage.
But equanimity is given
To the favorites of God. Thus they died
Both of them,   thus you saw them
Die, godly sorrow in your mighty soul.
And for this reason you dwell

                and in the holy night
Should someone consider the future and feel care
For the carefree sleep
Of children, fresh as flowers,
You come smiling, asking what he has
To fear where you are queen.

For you could never envy
The tender shoots of day,
You have always liked it
When sons are greater
Than their mother. You are never pleased
When elders look back

Ein Älteres spottet des Jüngern.
Wer denkt der theuern Väter
Nicht gern und erzählet
Von ihren Thaten,

          wenn aber Verwegnes geschah,
Und Undankbare haben
Das Ärgerniß   gegeben
Zu gerne blikt
Dann   zum
Und thatenscheu
Unendliche Reue und es haßt das Alte die Kinder.

Darum beschüze
Du Himmlische sie
Die jungen Pflanzen und wenn
Der Nord kömmt oder giftiger Thau weht oder
Zu lange dauert die Dürre
Und wenn sie üppigblühend
Versinken unter der Sense
Der allzuscharfen, gieb erneuertes Wachstum.
Und daß nur niemals nicht
Vielfältig, in schwachem Gezweige
Die Kraft mir vielversuchend
Zerstreue das frische Geschlecht, stark aber sei
Zu wählen aus Vielem das beste.

Nichts ists, das Böse. Das soll
Wie der Adler den Raub
Mir Eines begreifen.
Die Andern dabei. Damit sie nicht
Die Amme, die
Den Tag gebieret
Verwirren, falsch anklebend
Der Heimath und der Schwere spottend

And mock the young.
Who is not glad to remember
Ancestors and tell
Of their deeds,

　　　　　　　　　　but when things turned ugly
And the ungrateful ones
Brought　　　　　　　scandal
One looks all too gladly
Then　　　　　　toward
And deed-shy
Endless remorse and the old loathe children.

Therefore, heavenly one,
Protect them,
These young plants, and should
The northwind come, or poisonous dew,
Or should the drought go unabated
Or their exuberant bloom
Sink under the scythe,
All too sharp, give renewed growth.
And may the power that
Abounds in these feeble branches,
Enticing me in multifarious ways,
Never disperse this young race, but give it strength
To choose the best among many.

Evil is nothing. This should
Be grasped as eagle
His prey.
By everyone. Lest they
Disturb the nurse
Who gives birth
To the Day, while they falsely
Stick to home, jeering at hardship,

Der Mutter ewig sizen
Im Schoose. Denn groß ist
Von dem sie erben den Reichtum.
Der

Vor allem, daß man schone
Der Wildniß göttlichgebaut
Im reinen Geseze, woher
Es haben die Kinder
Des Gotts, lustwandelnd unter
Den Felsen und Haiden purpurn blühn
Und dunkle Quellen
Dir, o Madonna und
Dem Sohne, aber den anderen auch
Damit nicht, als von Knechten,
Mit Gewalt das ihre nehmen
Die Götter.

An den Gränzen aber, wo stehet
Der Knochenberg, so nennet man ihn
Heut, aber in alter Sprache heißet
Er Ossa, Teutoburg ist
Daselbst auch und voll geistigen Wassers
Umher das Land, da
Die Himmlischen all
Sich Tempel

Ein Handwerksmann.

Uns aber die wir
Daß

Und zu sehr zu fürchten die Furcht nicht!
Denn du nicht, holde

Never leaving their mother's
Lap. For his is great,
Whose wealth they inherit.
The

Above all, let the wilderness
Be spared, divinely built
According to pure laws, from which
God's children have it,
Roaming among rocks
And the purple meadows flower
And the dark springs
Are for you, Madonna, and
Your son, and for the others as well,
Lest the gods treat them
Like serfs, seizing what is theirs
By force.

But at the borders, where
The Knochenberg rises, as it is named
Today, but known in ancient tongue
As Ossa, here Teutoburg also
Lies and the surrounding countryside
Full of spirited waters, since
The gods all
Temples for themselves

A craftsman.

But to us, who
So that

Fear itself is not to be overfeared!
Not you, O gracious

aber es giebt
Ein finster Geschlecht, das weder einen Halbgott
Gern hört, oder wenn mit Menschen ein Himmlisches oder
In Woogen erscheint, gestaltlos, oder das Angesicht
Des reinen ehrt, des nahen
Allgegenwärtigen Gottes.

Doch wenn unheilige schon
        in Menge
           und frech

Was kümmern sie dich
O Gesang den Reinen, ich zwar
Ich sterbe, doch du
Gehest andere Bahn, umsonst
Mag dich ein Neidisches hindern.

Wenn dann in kommender Zeit
Du einem Guten begegnest
So grüß ihn, und er denkt,
Wie unsere Tage wohl
Voll Glüks, voll Leidens gewesen.
Von einem gehet zum andern

Noch Eins ist aber
Zu sagen. Denn es wäre
Mir fast zu plözlich
Das Glük gekommen,
Das Einsame, daß ich unverständig
Im Eigentum
Mich an die Schatten gewandt,
Denn weil du gabst
Den Sterblichen

but there exists
A somber race that does not gladly hear
Of demigods or of the divine appearing among men
Or waves, without a shape, nor does it honor the face
Of the pure, of the near
Everpresent God.

But when the profane
                   in mobs
                           brazenly

What do these matter to you,
O song, you are pure, whereas I,
I die, your course
Is different, envy
Cannot hope to hinder you.

Should you meet a good man
In times to come,
Simply greet him, and he will remember
How filled our days were
With joy, with sorrow.
One leads to the other

One more thing needs
Saying. For joy, lonely
Joy, might have overcome me
Almost too suddenly
So that, unable to fathom
What was mine,
I would have turned to the shades,
For since you gave
Mortals

Versuchend Göttergestalt,
Wofür ein Wort? so meint' ich, denn es hasset die Rede, wer
Das Lebenslicht das herzernährende sparet.
Es deuteten vor Alters
Die Himmlischen sich, von selbst, wie sie
Die Kraft der Götter hinweggenommen.

Wir aber zwingen
Dem Unglük ab und hängen die Fahnen
Dem Siegsgott, dem befreienden auf, darum auch
Hast du Räthsel gesendet. Heilig sind sie
Die Glänzenden, wenn aber alltäglich
Die Himmlischen und gemein
Das Wunder scheinen will, wenn nemlich
Wie Raub Titanenfürsten die Gaaben
Der Mutter greifen, hilft ein Höherer ihr.

The tempting shapes of gods
Why words? I thought, for speech is hateful
To one who conserves the heart-nourishing light of life.
In ancient times
Heavenly beings made sense of themselves and of how
They had made off with the strength of the gods.

But by force we obtain
From misfortune, and fly flags
For the god of victory, the liberator, which is why
You have sent enigmas. They are holy,
These radiant ones, but when
The heavenly appears a daily thing
Or the miracle seems common, when indeed
These Titan princes grab the Mother's gifts
As spoils, a higher power comes to her aid.

Die Titanen

Nicht ist es aber
Die Zeit. Noch sind sie
Unangebunden. Göttliches trift untheilnehmende nicht.
Dann mögen sie rechnen
Mit Delphi. Indessen, gieb in Feierstunden
Und daß ich ruhen möge, der Todten
Zu denken. Viele sind gestorben
Feldherrn in alter Zeit
Und schöne Frauen und Dichter
Und in neuer
Der Männer viel
Ich aber bin allein.

        und in den Ocean schiffend
Die duftenden Inseln fragen
Wohin sie sind.

Denn manches von ihnen ist
In treuen Schriften überblieben
Und manches in Sagen der Zeit.
Viel offenbaret der Gott.
Denn lang schon wirken
Die Wolken hinab
Und es wurzelt vielesbereitend heilige Wildniß.
Heiß ist der Reichtum. Denn es fehlet
An Gesang, der löset den Geist.
Verzehren würd' er
Und wäre gegen sich selbst
Denn nimmer duldet
Die Gefangenschaft das himmlische Feuer.

The Titans

The time has not yet
Come. They are still
At large. Those who take no part will not meet with gods.
Let them reckon with
Delphi. Meanwhile give me occasion to celebrate
And rest by thinking
Of the dead. Many generals
Died in ages past,
Beautiful women and poets too,
And in modern times,
Men, in droves,
I am alone.

                  and sailing the seas
Fragrant isles wonder
Where they've gone.

Something of them has faithfully
Survived in writing, and
Something in the legends of the time.
God reveals many things.
And clouds have long
Effected things below.
And the holy wilderness takes root, rich in promise.
So rich it burns. For we lack
Song to set the spirit loose.
It would turn against itself
And be consumed,
Godly fire cannot
Bear captivity.

Es erfreuet aber
Das Gastmahl oder wenn am Feste
Das Auge glänzet und von Perlen
Der Jungfrau Hals.
      Auch Kriegesspiel

                    und durch die Gänge
Der Gärten schmettert
Das Gedächtniß der Schlacht und besänftiget
An schlanker Brust
Die tönenden Wehre ruhn
Von Heldenvätern den Kindern.
Mich aber umsummet
Die Bien und wo der Akersmann
Die Furchen machet singen gegen
Dem Lichte die Vögel. Manche helfen
Dem Himmel. Diese siehet
Der Dichter. Gut ist es, an andern sich
Zu halten. Denn keiner trägt das Leben allein.

Wenn aber ist entzündet
Der geschäfftige Tag
Und an der Kette, die
Den Bliz ableitet
Von der Stunde des Aufgangs
Himmlischer Thau glänzt,
Muß unter Sterblichen auch
Das Hohe sich fühlen.
Drum bauen sie Häußer
Und die Werkstatt gehet
Und über Strömen das Schiff.
Und es bieten tauschend die Menschen
Die Händ' einander, sinnig ist es
Auf Erden und es sind nicht umsonst
Die Augen an den Boden geheftet.

But banquets
Give pleasure, or when eyes
Brighten at a feast, or a young
Girl's neck with pearls.
Games of war too

                        and through garden
Paths memories of battle
Crash, and clanging swords
Of heroic ancestors lie
Softly on children's
Slender breasts.
And bees buzz
Around me and where the ploughman
Sets his furrows, birds sing
Against the light. Some come
To heaven's help. These
The poet sees. It is good to lean
On others. No one can bear life alone.

But when the day's
Business is kindled
And the lightning
Chains sparkle
With dawn's
Heavenly dew,
Even mortals must feel
The presence of something higher.
Which is why they build houses
And run workshops
And send ships across the sea.
And men offer their hands
In exchange, the earth is absorbed
In thought, eyes cast
To the ground for good cause.

Ihr fühlet aber
Auch andere Art.
Denn unter dem Maaße
Des Rohen brauchet es auch
Damit das Reine sich kenne.
Wenn aber

Und in die Tiefe greifet
Daß es lebendig werde
Der Allerschütterer, meinen die
Es komme der Himmlische
Zu Todten herab und gewaltig dämmerts
Im ungebundenen Abgrund
Im allesmerkenden auf.
Nicht möcht ich aber sagen
Es werden die Himmlischen schwach
Wenn schon es aufgährt.
Wenn aber
          und es gehet

An die Scheitel dem Vater, daß

          und der Vogel des Himmels ihm
Es anzeigt. Wunderbar
Im Zorne kommet er drauf.

Yet you also feel
A presence of a different kind.
For gross things must also enter
The balance, if there is to be
Evidence of the pure.
But when

And the mover and shaker
Reaches into depths
To give life, they think
The god is going down
To the dead, and the abyss,
Unbound, all-fathoming,
Seethes with light.
Though I wouldn't want to say
The ferment
Weakens the gods.
But when
     and it goes

To the father's crown, so that

    and the bird of heaven
Points it out to him. Awesome
He appears in a rage.

[Einst hab ich die Muse gefragt . . .]

Einst hab ich die Muse gefragt, und sie
Antwortete mir
Am Ende wirst du es finden.
Kein Sterblicher kann es fassen.
Vom Höchsten will ich schweigen.
Verbotene Frucht, wie der Lorbeer, aber ist
Am meisten das Vaterland. Die aber kost'
Ein jeder zulezt,

Viel täuschet Anfang
Und Ende.
Das lezte aber ist
Das Himmelszeichen, das reißt
      und   Menschen
Hinweg. Wohl hat Herkules das
Gefürchtet. Aber da wir träge
Geboren sind, bedarf es des Falken, dem
Befolgt' ein Reuter, wenn
Er jaget, den Flug.

Im   wenn
Und der Fürst

        und Feuer und Rauchdampf blüht
Auf dürrem Rasen
Doch ungemischet darunter
Aus guter Brust, das Labsaal
Der Schlacht, die Stimme quillet des Fürsten.

[I once asked the muse . . .]

I once asked the muse, and she
Replied:
You will find it in the end.
No mortal can grasp it.
Of the Highest I will not speak.
But, above all, one's native land
Is forbidden fruit, like laurel. Of which
Everyone shall taste in the end,

Most deceptive are beginning
And end.
Yet the sign from heaven
Come last, it snatches
      and   men
Away. This is what Hercules
No doubt feared. But since we were born
Dull, falcons are needed
Whose flight horsemen
Follow on hunts.

In   when
And the Prince

      and fire and smoke flower
On the parched green,
But distinct from this, the voice
Of the Prince, soothing
The battle, surges from strong lungs.

Gefäße machet ein Künstler.
Und es kauffet

                     wenn es aber
Zum Urteil kommt
Und keusch hat es die Lippe
Von einem Halbgott berührt

Und schenket das Liebste
Den Unfruchtbaren
Denn nimmer, von nun an
Taugt zum Gebrauche das Heilge.

An artist makes vessels.
Bought by

                    but when it
Comes to judgment,
Chastely grazed
By some demigod's lips

And bestows what he loves most
Upon the barren,
For from now on, the sacred
Is no longer fit for use.

[Wenn aber die Himmlischen . . .]

Wenn aber die Himmlischen haben
Gebaut, still ist es
Auf Erden, und wohlgestalt stehn
Die betroffenen Berge. Gezeichnet
Sind ihre Stirnen. Denn es traf
Sie, da den Donnerer hielt
Unzärtlich die gerade Tochter
Des Gottes bebender Stral
Und wohl duftet gelöscht
Von oben der Aufruhr.
Wo inne stehet, beruhiget, da
Und dort,   das Feuer.
Denn Freude schüttet
Der Donnerer aus und hätte fast
Des Himmels vergessen
Damals im Zorne, hätt ihn nicht
Das Weise gewarnet.
Jezt aber blüht es
Am armen Ort.
Und wunderbar groß will
Es stehen.
Gebirg hänget   See,
Warme   Tiefe   es kühlen aber die Lüfte
Inseln und Halbinseln,
Grotten zu beten,

Ein glänzender Schild
Und schnell, wie Rosen,

                                    oder es schafft
Auch andere Art,
Es sprosset aber

[*But when the gods . . .*]

But when the gods have done
Building, silence comes over
The earth, and the mountains
Stand finely shaped, their features
Traced. For as the Thunderer
Contended with his daughter,
They were struck by
The god's trembling ray,
And fragrance descends
As the uproar wanes.
Where it lies within, soothes, here
And there   the fire.
For the Thunderer showers
Forth joy and would have
Almost forgotten heaven
In his wrath, had not
Wisdom given him warning.
But now even poor places
Are in flower.
And will rise
Majestic.
Mountain overhangs   lake,
Warm   deep   but breezes cool
Islands and peninsulas,
Grottoes for praying,

A sparkling shield,
And quick, as roses

                or else creates
Other ways,
But the sprouting of

                              viel üppig neidiges
Unkraut, das blendet, schneller schießet
Es auf, das ungelenke, denn es scherzet
Der Schöpferische, sie aber
Verstehen es nicht. Zu zornig greifft
Es und wächst. Und dem Brande gleich,
Der Häußer verzehret, schlägt
Empor, achtlos, und schonet
Den Raum nicht, und die Pfade bedeket,
Weitgährend, ein dampfend Gewölk
                              die unbeholfene Wildinß.
So will es göttlich scheinen. Aber
Furchtbar ungastlich windet
Sich durch den Garten die Irre,
Die augenlose, da den Ausgang
Mit reinen Händen kaum
Erfindet ein Mensch. Der gehet, gesandt,
Und suchet, dem Thier gleich, das
Nothwendige. Zwar mit Armen,
Der Ahnung voll, mag einer treffen
Das Ziel. Wo nemlich
Die Himmlischen eines Zaunes oder Merkmals,
Das ihren Weg
Anzeige, oder eines Bades
Bedürfen, reget es wie Feuer
In der Brust der Männer sich.

Noch aber hat andre
Bei sich der Vater.
Denn über den Alpen
Weil an den Adler
Sich halten müssen, damit sie nicht
Mit eigenem Sinne zornig deuten
Die Dichter, wohnen über dem Fluge
Des Vogels, un den Thron

rank envious
Weeds, deceptive as they shoot
Up quick and uncouth,
For the Creator has tricks
They do not understand. It grasps
And spreads with too much fury. And like fire
Consuming houses, lashes
Out, uncaring, and spares
No space and covers paths,
Seething everywhere, a smoldering cloud
                              wilderness without end.
Seeking to pass for something
Godly. But Error reels eyeless
Through the garden, dreadful,
Inhospitable, since no man
With clean hands can
Find exit. He proceeds, driven
Like a beast in search of
Necessities. Though with his arms
And premonitions, a man may reach
The goal. For where
The gods require fences or markers
To indicate their path,
Or need a pool to bathe,
The hearts of men
Beat like fire.

But the Father had others
By his side.
For above the Alps
Where poets must rely
Upon the eagle, lest their angry
Interpretations make mere private sense,
And living above the flight
Of birds, around the throne

Des Gottes der Freude
Und deken den Abgrund
Ihm zu, die gelbem Feuer gleich, in reißender Zeit
Sind über Stirnen der Männer,
Die Prophetischen, denen möchten
Es neiden, weil die Furcht
Sie lieben, Schatten der Hölle,

Sie aber trieb,
Ein rein Schiksaal
Eröffnend   von
Der Erde heiligen Tischen
Der Reiniger Herkules,
Der bleibet immer lauter, jezt noch,
Mit dem Herrscher, und othembringend steigen
Die Dioskuren ab und auf,
An unzugänglichen Treppen, wenn von himmlischer Burg
Die Berge fernhinziehen
Bei Nacht, und hin
Die Zeiten
Pythagoras

Im Gedächtniß aber lebet Philoktetes,

Die helfen dem Vater.
Denn ruhen mögen sie. Wenn aber
Sie reizet unnüz Treiben
Der Erd' und es nehmen
Den Himmlischen
                    die Sinne, brennend kommen
Sie dann,

Of the Lord of Joy
From whom they conceal
The abyss, these, the prophetic ones,
Lie above the gaze of men
Like yellow fire, in torn
Times, envied by those in love
With fear, the shades of hell,

But they were driven,
A pure fate
Opening   from
The sacred tables of the earth
Hercules the Purifier
Who remains undefiled to this day
With the Lord, and the breath-bearing
Dioscuri climb up and down
Inaccessible stairs as the mountains
Retreat from the heavenly fortress
At night, and gone
The times
Of Pythagoras.

Philoctetes lives in memory.

They go to the Father's aid
For they desire rest. But when
The useless doings of the earth
Provoke them and from the gods
Are taken
              senses, they then come
Burning

Die othemlosen

Denn es hasset
Der sinnende Gott
Unzeitiges Wachstum.

These without breath

For thoughtful God
Detests
Untimely growth.

[Sonst nemlich, Vater Zevs . . .]

Sonst nemlich, Vater Zevs

Denn

Jezt aber hast du
Gefunden anderen Rath

Darum geht schröklich über
Der Erde Diana
Die Jägerin und zornig erhebt
Unendlicher Deutung voll
Sein Antliz über uns
Der Herr. Indeß das Meer seufzt, wenn
Er kommt

O wär es möglich
Zu schonen mein Vaterland

Doch allzuscheu nicht,

Es würde   lieber sei
Unschiklich und gehe, mit der Erinnys, fort
Mein Leben.
Denn über der Erde wandeln
Gewaltige Mächte,
Und es ergreiffet ihr Schiksaal
Den der es leidet und zusieht,
Und ergreifft den Völkern das Herz.

Denn alles fassen muß
Ein Halbgott oder ein Mensch, dem Leiden nach,
Indem er höret, allein, oder selber
Verwandelt wird, fernahnend die Rosse des Herrn,

[*There was a time . . .*]

There was a time, Father Zeus

Because

But now you have
Found different counsel

Which is why the huntress
Diana stalks the earth
Inspiring dread and the angry
Lord raises his face
Over us, filled with
Infinite sense. While the ocean sighs
At his coming.

O were it possible
To spare my native land

Yet not be too timid

It would   rather
Give my own life, against all
Measure, to Erinys,
For powerful forces
Wander the earth,
Whose destiny is grasped
By those who witness it and suffer,
Grasping the people in their heart.

For a demigod or man
Must seize it all according to his suffering,
As he listens, alone, or is himself
Transformed, sensing the far horses of the Lord.

[Meinest du es solle gehen . . .]

meinest du
Es solle gehen,
Wie damals? Nemlich sie wollten stiften
Ein Reich der Kunst. Dabei ward aber
Das Vaterländische von ihnen
Versäumet und erbärmlich gieng
Das Griechenland, das schönste, zu Grunde.
Wohl hat es andere
Bewandtniß jezt.
Es sollten nemlich die Frommen

und alle Tage wäre
Das Fest.
Also darf nicht
Ein ehrlich Meister

und wie mit Diamanten
In die Fenster machte, des Müßiggangs wegen
Mit meinen Fingern, hindert

so hat mir
Das Kloster etwas genüzet,

[*Do you think . . .*]

                          do you think
Things will go
As they once did? They wanted to found
A kingdom of art. But in the process
Neglected what was native
To them, and Greece, fairest of all,
Went down pitifully.
The case is certainly
Different now.
Indeed, the devout should

                          and every day would be
A feast.
                             A respected teacher
Thus should not

                            and as with diamonds
Etched in windows by my idle
Fingers, hinders

                           so the cloister
Was of help to me,

Der Adler

Mein Vater ist gewandert, auf dem Gotthard.
Da wo die Flüsse, hinab,
Wohl nach Hetruria seitwärts,
Und des geraden Weges
Auch über den Schnee,
Zum Olympos und Hämos
Wo den Schatten der Athos wirft,
Nach Höhlen in Lemos.
Anfänglich aber sind
Aus Wäldern des Indus
Die Eltern gekommen.
Der Urahn aber
Ist geflogen über der See
Scharfsinnend, und es wunderte sich
Des Königs goldnes Haupt
Ob dem Geheimniß der Wasser,
Als roth die Wolken dampften
Über dem Schiff. Die Thiere stumm
Einander schauend
Der Speise gedachten, aber
Es stehen die Berge doch still,
Wo wollen wir bleiben?

Reh.

Der Fels ist zu Waide gut,
Das Trokne zu Trank.
Das Nasse aber zu Speise.
Will einer wohnen,
So sei es an Treppen,

The Eagle

My father roamed over the Gotthard
Where the rivers dive
Sideways toward Etruria
And flow straight
Over snow
To Olympos and Haimos,
Where Athos casts shadows,
To caves in Lemnos.
In the beginning,
Though, my parents arose
From the fragrant
Forests of the Indus.
And our first ancestor
Soared over the sea,
Keen in thought, and the king's
Golden head marveled
At the waters' secret
As red clouds steamed
Above the ark and animals
Stared dumbly at each other,
Thinking of feed. Yet
The mountains stand still,
Where shall we nest?

Deer.

Rock goes with pasture,
Dryness goes with drink.
But solid food needs washing down.
If you wish to settle,
Let it be by stairs,

Und wo ein Häuslein hinabhängt
Am Wasser halte dich auf.
Und was einer hat, ist
Athem zu hohlen.
Hat einer ihn nemlich hinauf
Am Tage gebracht,
Er findet im Schlaf ihn wieder.
Denn wo die Augen zugedekt,
Und gebunden die Füße sind,
Da wirst du es finden.

And where a cottage overhangs
The river, spend your days.
What you possess
Is taking breath.
What you raise
By day, rediscover
In sleep.
Where eyes are covered
And feet are bound,
You will find it.

[Ihr sichergebaueten Alpen . . .]

Ihr sichergebaueten Alpen!
Die

Und ihr sanftblikenden Berge,
Wo über buschigem Abhang
Der Schwarzwald saußt,
Und Wohlgerüche die Loke
Der Tannen herabgießt,
Und der Nekar

      und die Donau!
Im Sommer liebend Fieber
Umherwehet der Garten
Und Linden des Dorfs, und wo
Die Pappelweide blühet
Und der Seidenbaum
Auf heiliger Waide,

Und

Ihr guten Städte!
Nicht ungestalt, mit dem Feinde
Gemischet unmächtig

Was
Auf einmal gehet es weg
Und siehet den Tod nicht.
Wann aber

Und Stutgard, wo ich
Ein Augenbliklicher begraben

[Alps . . .]

Alps, built to endure!
O

Mountains gazing gently
Over bushy cliffs
Where the Black Forest whispers
And the pines pour forth
The scent of their hair,
And the Neckar

                 and the Danube!
Summer's loving fever
Floats through the lime trees
And gardens of the village, and where
The poplar blooms
And the mulberry tree
On sacred meadow

And

O excellent towns!
Not misshapen or helplessly
Mingling with the enemy

What
It disappears at once
Nor sees death.
But when

And Stuttgart where I,
Creature of the moment,

Liegen dürfte, dort,
Wo sich die Straße
Bieget, und
        um die Weinstaig,
Und der Stadt Klang wieder
Sich findet drunten auf ebenem Grün
Stilltönend unter den Apfelbäumen

Des Tübingens   wo
und Blize fallen
Am hellen Tage
Und Römisches tönend ausbeuget der Spizberg
Und Wohlgeruch

Und Tills Thal, das

Could lie buried,
There, at the bend
In the road and
            near the Weinsteig
Down where the town comes back
Into hearing on the green valley floor,
Quietly sounding through the apple trees

Of Tübingen   where
And lightning strikes
In broad daylight
And the Spitzberg curves off, resonant with Roman things
And fragrance

And Thill's valley which

Das Nächste Beste

offen die Fenster des Himmels
Und freigelassen der Nachtgeist
Der himmelstürmende, der hat unser Land
Beschwäzet, mit Sprachen viel, unbändigen, und
Den Schutt gewälzet
Bis diese Stunde.
Doch kommt das, was ich will,
Wenn

Drum wie die Staaren
Mit Freudengeschrei, wenn auf Gasgone, Orten, wo viel Gärten,
Wenn im Olivenland Springbrunnen und
In liebenswürdiger Fremde die Bäum
An grasbewachsnen Wegen
Unwissend in der Wüste
Die Sonne sticht,
Und das Herz der Erde thuet
Sich auf, wo um
Den Hügel von Eichen
Aus brennendem Lande
Die Ströme und wo
Des Sonntaags unter Tänzen
Gastfreundlich die Schwellen sind,
An blüthenbekränzten Straßen, stillegehend.
Sie spüren nemlich die Heimath,
Wenn grad aus falbem Stein
Die Wasser silbern rieseln
Und heilig Grün sich zeigt
Auf feuchter Wiese der Charente,

The Nearest the Best

                    the windows of heaven are open,
The spirit of night is on the loose,
Who takes the sky by storm and has confounded
Our land with a babble of tongues, and
Stirred up rubble
To this very day.
But my wishes will be realized
When

Thus like starlings
With screams of joy, when above Gascogne, regions of countless
          gardens,
When fountains, where olives grow
On lovely foreign soil, when trees
By grassy paths
Unaware in the wild
Are stung by the sun,
And earth's heart
Opens, where rivers
From the burning plain
Flow around hills
Of oak, where
Sundays, amid dancing,
Thresholds offer welcome and
Blossoms wreathe the quiet procession of streets.
They sense their native land,
When the silver waters trickle
 From pale yellow rock
And the holiness of green is revealed
On the moist meadows of the Charente,

Die klugen Sinne pflegend.   wenn aber,
Die Luft sich bahnt,
Und ihnen machet waker
Scharfwehend die Augen der Nordost, fliegen sie auf,
Und Ek um Eke
Das Liebere gewahrend
Denn immer halten die sich genau an das Nächste,
Sehn sie die heiligen Wälder und die Flamme, blühendduftend
Des Wachstums und die Wolken des Gesanges fern und athmen
        Othem
Der Gesänge. Menschlich ist
Das Erkenntniß. Aber die Himmlischen
Auch haben solches mit sich und des Morgens beobachten
Die Stunden und des Abends die Vögel. Himmlischen auch
Gehöret also solches. Wolan nun. Sonst in Zeiten
Des Geheimnisses hätt ich, als von Natur, gesagt,
Sie kommen, in Deutschland. Jezt aber, weil, wie die See
Die Erd ist und die Länder, Männern gleich, die nicht
Vorüber gehen können, einander, untereinander
Sich schelten fast, so sag ich. Abendlich wohlgeschmiedet
Vom Oberlande biegt sich das Gebrig, wo auf hoher Wiese die
        Wälder sind
Wohl an der bairischen Ebne. Nemlich Gebirg
Geht weit und streket, hinter Amberg sich und
Fränkischen Hügeln. Berühmt ist dieses. Umsonst nicht hat
Seitwärts gebogen Einer von Bergen der Jugend
Das Gebirg, und gerichtet das Gebirg
Heimatlich. Wildniß nemlich sind ihm die Alpen und
Das Gebirg, das theilet die Tale und die Länge nach
Geht über die Erd. Dort aber

            und rauschen, über spizem Winkel
Frohlokende Bäume. Gut ist, das gesezt ist. Aber Eines
Das ficht uns an. Anhang, der bringt uns fast um heiligen Geist.

Cultivating keen senses.   but when
The breeze carves its way
And the sharp northeasterly
Quickens their eyes, they fly up,
And at every corner
Lovelier things draw into their sight,
For they cleave to what is nearest,
And see the sacred forests and the flame of growth
In fragrant flower and the distant choirs of clouds breathe in
The breath of songs. Recognition
Is human. But the gods
Have this in them too, and observe the hours
At dawn and birds at dusk. So this
Also pertains to the gods. Well, fine. There was a secret
Time when by nature I would have said
They were coming to Germany. But now, since the earth
Is like the sea, and the nations, like men who cannot
Cross to each other's coasts, squabble
Among themselves, I speak as follows. To the west, well-forged,
The mountains curve down from the uplands where woods on
        high meadows
Overlook the Bavarian plain. For the range
Reaches far, stretching beyond Amberg and
The Franconian hills. This is well known. Not for nothing
Did someone curve the range away from the mountains
Of youth and face it
Homewards. To him the Alps are a wilderness and
The mountains that sever valleys, strung lengthwise
Across the earth. But there

                    and trees rejoice and rustle over the peaked
Shelter. What is in place is good. But one thing
We grapple with. It hangs on, nearly depriving us of the holy
        spirit.

Barbaren
Auch leben, wo allein herrschet Sonne
Und Mond. Gott aber hält uns, wenn zu sehn ist einer, der wolle
Umkehren mein Vaterland.

Gehn mags nun. Der Rosse Leib
War der Geist. Bei Ilion aber auch
Das Licht der Adler. Aber in der Mitte
Der Himmel der Gesänge. Neben aber,
Am Ufer zorniger Greise, der Entscheidung nemlich, die alle
Drei unser sind.

Barbarians also live where the sun and moon
Reign alone. But God sustains us, if indeed there be one, would
that
He change my fatherland around.

Now, to move on. The spirit was
The horse's flesh. But at Ilion
Was also the light of eagles. But in the middle
The heaven of songs. But next to this,
Angry old men, on the shore of judgment,
All three of which ours.

Tinian

Süß ists, zu irren
In heiliger Wildniß,

Und an der Wölfin Euter, o guter Geist,
Der Wasser, die
Durchs heimatliche Land
Mir irren,

        , wilder sonst,
Und jezt gewöhnt, zu trinken, Findlingen gleich;
Des Frühlings, wenn im warmen Grunde
Des Haines wiederkehrend fremde Fittige

                ausruhend in Einsamkeit,
Und an Palmtagsstauden
Wohlduftend
Mit Sommervögeln
Zusammenkommen die Bienen,
Und deinen Alpen

Von Gott getheilet

Der Welttheil,

              zwar sie stehen
Gewapnet,

Und lustzuwandeln, zeitlos

Tinian

Pleasant to stray
Through holy wilderness,

O kindly spirit, and at the wolf teats
Of the waters which meander
Across my native land
To me,

                   , wilder once,
But now accustomed to nurse as foundlings do;
In springtime, when foreign wings
Return to the warm depth of the woods

                        finding rest in solitude,
And among the fragrant
Willow trees
The bees meet
With butterflies,
And your Alps

Parted by God

Part of the world,

                   though they rise
Armored,

And to roam at will, timeless

                    denn es haben
Wie Wagenlauff uns falkenglänzend, oder
Dem Thierskampf gleich, als Muttermaal
Weß Geistes Kind
Die Abendländischen sein, die Himmlischen
Uns diese Zierde geordnet;

                        Die Blumen giebt es,
Nicht von der Erde gezeugt, von selber
Aus lokerem Boden sprossen die,
Ein Widerstral des Tages, nicht ist
Es ziemend, diese zu pflüken,
Denn golden stehen,
Unzubereitet,
Ja schon die unbelaubten
Gedanken gleich,

                                   for the gods
Who glint at us like hawks,
Have decreed that,
Like gladiators or charioteers,
Such adornment be our birthmark
To show whose child the West might be;

                                There are flowers
Not engendered by the earth, sprouting
From loose soil of their own accord,
Day's counterlight, it is not
Proper to pick these,
For they stand golden,
Unprepared,
Without leaves,
Like thoughts,

Kolomb

Wünscht' ich der Helden einer zu seyn
Und dürfte frei, mit der Stimme des Schäfers, oder eines Hessen,
Dessen eingeborner Sprach, es bekennen
So wär' es ein Seeheld. Thätigkeit, zu gewinnen nemlich
Ist das freundlichste, das
Unter allen

Heimische Wohnung und Ordnung, durchaus bündig,
Dürre Schönheit zu lernen und Gestalten
In den Sand gebrannt
Aus Nacht und Feuer, voll von Bildern, reingeschliffenes
Fernrohr, hohe Bildung, nemlich für das Leben
Den Himmel zu fragen.

Wenn du sie aber nennest
Anson und Gama, Äneas
Und Jason, Chirons
Schüler in Megaras Felsenhöhlen, und
Im zitternden Reegen der Grotte bildete sich ein Menschenbild
Aus Eindrüken des Walds, und die Tempelherren, die gefahren
Nach Jerusalem Bouillon, Rinaldo,
Bougainville   [Entdekungsreisen
als versuche, den hesperischen
orbis gegen den
orbis der Alten zu bestimmen]

Gewaltig ist die Zahl
Gewaltiger aber sind sie selbst
Und machen stumm

                      die Männer.
Dennoch

Columbus

If there were a hero I wanted to be
And were free to say so with shepherd's voice
Or a Hessian's native speech,
It would be a hero of the sea. Action, to achieve this
Is friendliest
Of all

A home and domestic order absolutely essential
To learning the beauty of deserts and figures
Burnt into sand
Out of night and fire, full of images, a telescope
With keen lens and considerable education if life
Is to question the heavens.

But when you name them over
Anson and Gama, Aeneas
And Jason, the pupil
Of Chiron in Megara's caves, and
In the grotto's quivering rain a human image took shape
From impressions of the forest, and the Templars who sailed
Toward Jerusalem, Bouillon, Rinaldo,
Bougainville [voyages of discovery
as attempts to define
the Hesperidean orbis as
against that of the ancients]

Their number is great
But they themselves are greater
And strike men

                              dumb
Nonetheless

Und hin nach Genua will ich
Zu erfragen Kolombos Haus
Wo er, als wenn
Eins der Götter eines wäre und wunderbar
Der Menschen Geschlecht,
In süßer Jugend gewohnet. Licht
Aber man kehret
Wesentlich um, wie ein
Bildermann, der stehet
Vorm Kornhaus, von Sicilien her vieleicht
Und die Bilder weiset der Länder
Der Großen auch
Und singet der Welt Pracht,

                              so du
Mich aber fragest

So weit das Herz
Mir reichet, wird es gehen
Nach Brauch und Kunst.

Zu Schiffe aber steigen
ils crient rapport, il fermes maison
tu es un saisrien

Ein Murren war es, ungedultig, denn
Von wengen geringen Dingen
Verstimmt wie vom Schnee ward
Die Erde zornig und eilte, während daß sie schrien
Manna und Himmelsbrod

And I want to go to Genoa
And inquire after the house of Columbus
Where, as though a man
Might be a god and
Humankind a marvel,
He spent his sweet youth. Light
But essentially
One turns back, like a
Picture vendor, perhaps from Sicily,
Who stands in front of a granary
And displays images of countries
And continents
And sings the splendors of the earth,

                    but since
You ask me

As far as my heart
Reaches, things will go
According to custom and art.

But boarding the ships
ils crient rapport, il fermes maison
tu es un saisrien

There was impatient grumbling, for
As though thrown out of tune
By snowfall, these trifles
Angered the earth to hasten
Toward supper, as they shouted
Manna and bread from heaven

Mit Prophezeiungen und
Großem Geschrei, des Gebets mit Gunst,
Zum Abendessen.
Sauer wird mir dieses wenig
Geduld und Gütigkeit mein Richter und Schuzgott
Denn Menschen sind wir
Und sie glaubten, sie seien Mönche.
Und einer, als Redner
Auftrat uns als Pfarherr
Im blauen Wamms

entiere personne content de son
ame difficultes connoissance
rapport tire

Doch da hinaus, damit
Vom Plaze
Wir kommen, also rief
Gewaltig richtend
Die Gesellen die Stimme des Meergotts,
Die reine, daran
Heroen erkennen, ob sie recht
Gerathen oder nicht

Stürzet herein, ihr Bäche
Von Lieb und Gottes Gnad und Glük im seinen,
Kräfte zu begreiffen, o ihr Bilder
Der Jugend, als in Genua, damals
Der Erdkreis, griechisch, kindlich gestalte,
Mit Gewalt unter meinen Augen,
Einschläfernd, kurzgefaßtem Mohngeist gleich mir
Erschien

Das bist du ganz in deiner Schönheit apocalyptica.

With prophesying and great
Commotion, with supplication
And prayer.
Such lack of grace and patience
Is bitter to me, my judge and guardian god,
For we are men
And they believed themselves monks.
And one, an orator,
Took the floor, a priest or captain
In a blue jacket

entiere personne content de son
ame difficultes connoisance
rapport tire

Yet out there, calling
Us from
This place, powerfully
Commanding the crew,
Came the pure voice
Of the seagod, by which
Heroes recognize whether
Or not they will succeed

Plunge in, O streams
Of love and luck by the grace of God,
To comprehend the powers, O images
Of youth, the way the world appeared
To me back then in Genoa, mapped
By a child or Greek,
Surging beneath my sleepy lids like a fleeting
Poppy dream

You are all this in your beauty apocalyptica

moments tirees hautes sommeils der Schiffer
Kolombus aber beiseit Hypostasierung des vorigen orbis
Naiveté der Wissenschaft
Und seufzeten miteinander, um die Stunde,
Nach der Hizze des Tags.
lui a les pleures

Sie sahn nun

Es waren nemlich viele,
Der schönen Inseln.

               damit
Mit Lissabon

Und Genua theilten;

Denn einsam kann
Von Himmlischen den Reichtum tragen
Nicht eins; wohl nemlich mag
Den Harnisch dehnen
            ein Halbgott, dem Höchsten aber
Ist fast zu wenig
Das Wirken   wo das Tagslicht scheinet,
Und der Mond,

       Darum auch

          so

Nemlich öfters, wenn
Den Himmlischen zu einsam
Es wird, daß sie
Allein zusammenhalten

moments tirees hautes sommeils, the sailor
Columbus aside, the previous orbis hypostatized
Naiveté of science
And they sighed among themselves, at the hour
After the heat of day
lui a les pleures

They now saw

And indeed there were many
Lovely isles.

                    so that
split between Lisbon

And Genoa;

For no one can
Bear the wealth of the heavens
All alone; though some demigod
Might well loosen
                    the reins, for the Highest
Such action is hardly
Enough   where daylight shines
And the moon,

            Which is also why

                    so

Often, when
It gets too lonely
For the gods, so that
They huddle together alone

oder die Erde; denn allzurein ist

Entweder

Dann aber

die Spuren der alten Zucht,

or the earth; far too pure is

Either

But then

traces of the ancient breed,

[Und mitzufühlen das Leben . . .]

Und mitzufühlen das Leben
Der Halbgötter oder Patriarchen, sizend
Zu Gericht. Nicht aber überall ists
Ihnen gleich um diese, sondern Leben, summendheißes auch vor
      Schatten Echo
Als in einen Brennpunct
Versammelt. Goldne Wüste. Oder wohlunterhalten dem
      Feuerstahl des lebenswarmen
Heerds gleich schlägt dann die Nacht Funken, aus geschliffnem
      Gestein
Des Tages, und um die Dämmerung noch
Ein Saitenspiel tönt. Gegen das Meer zischt
Der Knall der Jagd. Die Aegypterin aber, offnen Busens sizt
Immer singend wegen Mühe gichtisch das Gelenk
Im Wald, am Feuer. Recht Gewissen bedeutend
Der Wolken und der Seen des Gestirns
Rauscht in Schottland wie an dem See
Lombardas dann ein Bach vorüber. Knaben spielen
Perlfrischen Lebens gewohnt so um Gestalten
Der Meister, oder der Leichen, oder es rauscht so um der Thürme
      Kronen
Sanfter Schwalben Geschrei.

Nein wahrhaftig der Tag
Bildet keine
Menschenformen. Aber erstlich
Ein alter Gedanke, Wissenschaft
Elysium.

               und verlorne Liebe
Der Turniere   Rosse, scheu und feucht

[And to experience . . .]

And to experience what it is
Demigods or patriarchs feel, sitting
In judgment. Yet they are not equal to everything
In their surroundings, i.e., life, buzzing with heat and the echo
     of shadows
As if gathered to
The burning point. Golden wastelands. Or well-maintained, like
     the steel flint that lights the life-warm
Hearth, night suddenly strikes sparks from the polished stone
Of day, while a lyre
Plays around dusk. Hunter's gunshots
Whizz against the sea. But the Egyptian, her breasts bared, sits
And goes on singing, her joints gouty with grief,
In the woods, by the fire. Signifying clear conscience
Of the planet's clouds and seas
A stream rushes through Scotland
As toward the lakes of Lombardy. Seasoned to a life
As fresh as pearl, boys romp about the figures
Of their teachers, or of corpses, or swallows wheel around the
     crowns
Of towers, softly crying.

No, truly, the Day
Fashions no
Human shapes. But first,
An ancient notion, science
Elysium.

           and lost love
Of tournaments   horses, skittish and moist

[Reif sind . . .]

Reif sind, in Feuer getaucht, gekochet
Die Frücht und auf der Erde geprüfet und ein Gesez ist
Daß alles hineingeht, Schlangen gleich,
Prophetisch, träumend auf
Den Hügeln des Himmels. Und vieles
Wie auf den Schultern eine
Last von Scheitern ist
Zu behalten. Aber bös sind
Die Pfade. Nemlich unrecht,
Wie Rosse, gehn die gefangenen
Element' und alten
Geseze der Erd. Und immer
Ins Ungebundene gehet eine Sehnsucht. Vieles aber ist
Zu behalten. Und Noth die Treue.
Vorwärts aber und rükwärts wollen wir
Nicht sehn. Uns wiegen lassen, wie
Auf schwankem Kahne der See.

[*The fruits are ripe . . .*]

The fruits are ripe, dipped in fire, cooked
And tested here on earth, and it is a law,
Prophetic, that all things pass
Like snakes, dreaming on
The hills of heaven. And as
A load of logs upon
The shoulders, there is much
To bear in mind. But the paths
Are evil. For like horses,
The captive elements
And ancient laws
Of the earth go astray. Yet always
The longing to reach beyond bounds. But much
To be retained. And loyalty a must.
But we shall not look forward
Or back. Let ourselves rock, as
On a boat, lapped by the waves.

[Vom Abgrund nemlich . . .]

Vom Abgrund nemlich haben
Wir angefangen und gegangen
Dem Leuen gleich, in Zweifel und Ärgerniß,
Denn sinnlicher sind Menschen
In dem Brand
Der Wüste
Lichttrunken und der Thiergeist ruhet
Mit ihnen. Bald aber wird, wie ein Hund, umgehn
In der Hizze meine Stimme auf den Gassen der Gärten
In denen wohnen Menschen
In Frankreich
Der Schöpfer
Frankfurt aber, nach der Gestalt, die
Abdruk ist der Natur zu reden
Des Menschen nemlich, ist der Nabel
Dieser Erde, diese Zeit auch
Ist Zeit, und deutschen Schmelzes.
Ein wilder Hügel aber stehet über dem Abhang
Meiner Gärten. Kirschenbäume. Scharfer Othem aber wehet
Um die Löcher des Felses. Allda bin ich
Alles miteinander. Wunderbar
Aber über Quellen beuget schlank
Ein Nußbaum und   sich. Beere, wie Korall
Hängen an dem Strauche über Röhren von Holz,
Aus denen
Ursprünglich aus Korn, nun aber zu gestehen, bevestigter
        Gesang von Blumen als
Neue Bildung aus der Stadt, wo
Bis zu Schmerzen aber der Nase steigt
Citronengeruch auf und das Öl, aus der Provence, und es haben
        diese
Dankbarkeit mir die Gasgognischen Lande

[We set out from the abyss . . .]

We set out from the abyss
And proceeded like the lion,
Vexed with doubt,
Since men sense more
In the scorch
Of deserts,
Drunk with light, and the spirit of animals
Rests with them. But soon, like a dog in hot weather,
My voice shall amble through alleys of gardens
In which people live
In France.
The Creator.
But Frankfurt, to speak of man
By nature's stamp upon
The human shape, is the navel
Of this earth, and this age
Is time of German fusion.
A wild hill looms over the slope
Of my gardens. Cherry trees. And sharp breath blows
Through rock's holes. Here I am everything
At once. A lovely
Nut tree bends slender
Over springs and   itself. Berries, like coral,
Hang from shrubs over wooden pipes
Out of which
First from grain, now from flowers, fortified song
As new culture from the city, where nostrils
Nearly ache with the rising
Scent of lemon and oil from Provence, such gratitude
Have the lands of Gascogne

Gegeben. Gezähmet aber, noch zu sehen, und genährt hat mic
Die Rappierlust und des Festtags gebraten Fleisch
Der Tisch und braune Trauben, braune
                 und mich leset o
Ihr Blüthen von Deutschland, o mein Herz wird
Untrügbarer Krystall an dem
Des Licht sich prüfet wenn   Deutschland

Granted me. I have been tamed (still to be seen) and nourished
By love of rapier and festivals' roasted meats,
The table, the brown grapes, brown
                              and you gather me, O
Flowers of Germany, O my heart turns
Into unerring crystal, touchstone
Of light when   Germany

[Der Vatikan . . .]

der Vatikan,
Hier sind wir   in der Einsamkeit
Und drunten gehet der Bruder, ein Esel auch dem braunen Schleie
  nach
Wenn aber der Tag   ,allbejahend von wegen des Spott
Schiksaale macht, denn aus Zorn der Natur-
Göttin, wie ein Ritter gesagt von Rom, in derlei
Pallästen, gehet izt viel Irrsaal, und alle Schlüssel des
  Geheimnisses wissend
Fragt bös Gewissen
Und Julius Geist um derweil, welcher Calender
Gemachet, und dort drüben, in Westphalen,
Mein ehrlich Meister.
Gott rein und mit Unterscheidung
Bewahren, das ist uns vertrauet,
Damit nicht, weil an diesem
Viel hängt, über der Büßung, über einem Fehler
Des Zeichens
Gottes Gericht entstehet.
Ach! kennet ihr den nicht mehr
Den Meister des Forsts, und den Jüngling in der Wüste, der von
  Honig
Und Heuschreken sich nährt. Still Geists ists. Fraun
                          Oben wohl
Auf Monte   , wohl auch seitwärts,
Irr ich herabgekommen
Über Tyrol, Lombarda, Loretto, wo des Pilgrims Heimath
              auf dem Gotthard, gezäunt, nachlässig, unter
                  Gletschern
Karg wohnt jener, wo der Vogel
Mit Eiderdünnen, eine Perle des Meers
Und der Adler den Accent rufet, vor Gott, wo das Feuer läuft
  der Menschen wegen

[The Vatican . . .]

                    the Vatican,
Here we are   in solitude
And the monk walks down below, brown cloak followed by
    donkey.
But when the Day   , all-affirming to the point
    of derision,
Shapes destinies, for by the wrath of goddess
Nature, as a knight once said of the palaces of Rome,
There now reigns great confusion, and knowing all the keys to
    the secret,
Evil conscience casts its doubts,
And the spirit of Julius, who established
The calendar, meanwhile ranges about, according to my
    respected master
Over in Westphalia.
To keep God pure and maintain distinctions
Is entrusted us
Lest, and much depends
On this, penitence or a misconstrued
Sign
Bring down his judgment.
Ah, have you forgotten him,
The lord of the forest, the young man in the desert who lives
On locusts and honey? Quiet spirit. Women
                        Up above
On Monte   , and even sideways
I stray, down
Over Tyrol, Lombardy, Loreto, home of the pilgrim
            on the Gotthard, cloistered among glaciers, living
A lean life of ease, where the bird
With the eiderdown, pearl of the sea,
And the eagle shouts the accent, in the van of God, where fire
    streams on man's account,

Des Wächters Horn tönt aber über den Garden
Der Kranich hält die Gestalt aufrecht
Die Majestätische, keusche, drüben
In Patmos, Morea, in der Pestluft.
Türkisch. und die Eule, wohlbekannt der Schriften
Spricht, heischern Fraun gleich in zerstörten Städten. Aber
Die erhalten den Sinn. Oft aber wie ein Brand
Entstehet Sprachverwirrung. Aber wie ein Schiff,
Das lieget im Hafen, des Abends, wenn die Gloke lautet
Des Kirchthurms, und es nachhallt unten
Im Eingewaid des Tempels und der Mönch
Und Schäfer Abschied nehmet, vom Spaziergang
Und Apollon, ebenfalls
Aus Roma, derlei Pallästen, sagt
Ade! unreinlich bitter, darum!
Dann kommt das Brautlied des Himmels.
Vollendruhe. Goldroth. Und die Rippe tönet
Des sandigen Erdballs in Gottes Werk
Ausdrüklicher Bauart, grüner Nacht
Und Geist, der Säulenordnung, wirklich
Ganzem Verhältniß, samt der Mitt,
Und glänzenden

But the watchman's horn sounds out above the guards,
The crane holds his body high,
Chaste, majestic, far off
In Patmos, Morea, in the pestilent air.
Turkish. And the owl, familiar from Scripture, speaks
Like the wail of women in devastated towns. But
The sense is within their keeping. Often, though,' confusion of
       tongues
Breaks out like wildfire. But like a ship
Lying in port, at evening, when churchbells
Ring from the steeple and echo down
Into the bowels of the temple, and the monk
And shepherd part after a walk
And Apollo likewise says a bitter
Adieu to the unclean palaces
Of Rome, so
The bridesong of heaven begins.
Consummate peace. Golden red. And the coasts
Of this sandy globe resound to the express
Design of God, architect of green night
And spirit, and the order of columns, a work
Of total proportion, including the center,
Radiant

Griechenland

O ihr Stimmen des Geschiks, ihr Wege des Wanderers!
Denn an der Schule Blau, wo Geist von lang her toset,
Tönt wie Amsel Gesang
Der Wolken heitere Stimmung gut
Gestimmt vom Daseyn Gottes, dem Gewitter.
Und Rufer, wie wenn hinausschauen, zur
Unsterblichkeit und Helden;
Viel sind Erinnerungen. Wo darauf
Tönend, wie des Kalbs Haut
Die Erde, von Verwüstungen her, Versuchungen der Heiligen,
Großen Gesezen nachgeht,
Denn anfangs bildet das Werk sich Wissenschaft, die Einigkeit
Und Zärtlichkeit und den Himmel breit lauter Hülle nachher
Erscheinend singen,
Sterbende nemlich müssen singen, zierend den Geist des
          Himmels aber singen daselbst
Gesangeswolken. Denn immer lebt
Die Natur. Fest aber ist der Erde
Nabel. Gefangen nemlich in Ufern von Gras sind
Die Flammen und die allgemeinen
Elemente. Lauter Besinnung aber oben lebt der Äther. Aber
          silbern
An reinen Tagen
Ist das Licht. Als Zeichen der Liebe
Veilchenblau die Erde. Aber wo zu sehr
Zur Ewigkeit sich das Ungebundene sehnet
Himmlisches einschläft, und die Treue Gottes,
Das Verständige fehlt.
Aber wie der Reigen
Zur Hochzeit,
Zu Geringem auch kann kommen
Großer Anfang.
Alltag aber wunderbar zu lieb den Menschen
Gott an hat ein Gewand.

Greece

Voices of fate, roads travelers take!
In the school's open air, amid the spirit's old commotion,
The clear tempered clouds
Carry like the blackbird's call, well-
Tuned by the thunder, by God being there.
And cries ring out, as to catch sight
Of heroes and immortal life;
The memories are many. And
Vibrate, like a drumskin,
With all the ravages, all the temptations of saints from which
The earth proceeds, obeying mighty laws,
For the work of knowledge takes shape in the beginning, and
     the harmony
And tenderness and open sky which then
Appear, enveloping all things,
Are sung by choirs of clouds, though mortals should be the ones
     to sing,
Adorning the spirit of heaven. Nature
Lives forever. But the navel of the earth
Is firm. For the flames and universal
Elements are captive in the shore
Grass. But aether, sheer consciousness, lives above. On clear
Days the light
Is silver. The earth, a violet's blue
As a sign of love. But where
The longing for eternity knows no bounds,
Divine things are overcome with sleep, there is no trust
In God, no sense of proportion.
But like the round dance
At a wedding,
Great beginnings can come
To the smallest things.
Marvel of the common day,
God wears guises for man's sake.

Und Erkenntnissen verberget sich sein Angesicht
Und deket die Lüfte mit Kunst.
Und Luft und Zeit dekt
Den Schröklichen, daß zu sehr nicht eins
Ihn liebet mit Gebeten oder
Der Seele. Denn lange schon steht offen
Wie Blätter, zu lernen, oder Linien und Winkel die Natur.
Und gelber die Sonnen und Monde,
Zu Zeiten aber
Wenn ausgehn will die alte Bildung
Der Erde, bei Geschichten nemlich
Gewordnen, muthig fechtenden, wie auf Höhen führet
Die Erde Gott. Ungemessene Schritte
Begränzt er aber, wie Blüthen golden thun
Die Kräfte sich der Seele zusammen,
Daß lieber auf Erden
Die Schönheit wohnt und irgend ein Geist
Gemeinschaftlicher sich zu Menschen gesellet.

Süß ists dann unter hohen Schatten von Bäumen
Und Hügeln zu wohnen, sonnig, wo der Weg ist
Gepflastert zur Kirche,
Und Bäume stehen schlummernd, doch
Eintreffen Schritte der Sonne,
Denn eben so, wie heißer
Brennt über der Städte Dampf
So gehet über des Reegens
Behangene   Mauren   die Sonne

Wie Epheu nemlich hänget
Astlos der Reegen herunter. Schöner aber
Blühn Reisenden die Wege, wem
Aus Lebensliebe, messend immerhin,
Die Füße gehorchen, im Freien, wo das Land wechselt wie Korn.
Avignon waldig über den Gotthardt
Tastet das Roß, Lorbeern

And hides his face from recognitions
And veils the breezes with art.
And time and air conceal
His awesomeness, lest he be loved
Too much in soul
Or prayer. For nature has long lain
Open to learning, like leaves or lines or angles.
And yellower the sun and moons
At times
When the ancient civilization of the world
Threatens to go out, amid the blaze of battle,
And the old stories all come true, God then leads
The earth onto heights. But he limits
Unmeasured steps, and like blossoms,
The strengths of the soul cluster in gold,
So that beauty might elect
Residence on earth and a spirit of some kind
Seek the closer company of man.

It is then a lovely thing to live in the sun
Beneath the high shade of trees and hills where the path
To church is paved,
And trees drowse, despite
The tread of the sun,
For just as it burns hotter
Above city smoke,
So the sun moves above
Hung   walls   of rain

Like ivy, the rain hangs
Without branching. But roads
Bear finer bloom to travelers
Whose feet, for love of life, comply in measured
Stride, in the open, where the countryside sways like grain.
The horse picks his way toward woody Avignon
Beyond the Gotthard, a rustle

Rauschen um Virgilius und daß
Die Sonne nicht
Unmänlich suchet, das Grab. Moosrosen
Wachsen
Auf den Alpen. Blumen fangen
Vor Thoren der Stadt an, auf geebneten Wegen unbegünstiget
Gleich Krystallen in der Wüste wachsend des Meeres.
Gärten wachsen um Windsor. Hoch
Ziehet, aus London,
Der Wagen des Königs.
Schöne Gärten sparen die Jahrzeit.
Am Canal. Tief aber liegt
Das ebene Weltmeer, glühend.

Of laurels around Vergil
Shades the unmanly sun
From his grave. Moss roses
Grow
On the Alps. The flowers begin by the roadside
Beyond the city gates, as untended
As crystals growing in the wilds of the sea.
Gardens flourish around Windsor. The King's
Carriage drives up
From London.
Fine gardens save the season.
By the canal. But the ocean lies
Level, deep, and lambent.

[Was ist der Menschen Leben . . .]

Was ist der Menschen Leben   ein Bild der Gottheit.
Wie unter dem Himmel wandeln die Irrdischen alle, sehen
Sie diesen. Lesend aber gleichsam, wie
In einer Schrift, die Unendlichkeit nachahmen und den
      Reichtum
Menschen. Ist der einfältige Himmel
Denn reich? Wie Blüthen sind ja
Silberne Wolken. Es regnet aber von daher
Der Thau und das Feuchte. Wenn aber
Das Blau ist ausgelöschet, das Einfältige, scheint
Das Matte, das dem Marmelstein gleichet, wie Erz,
Anzeige des Reichtums.

[What is the life of man . . .]

What is the life of man? An image of divinity.
As they all wander beneath the sky, mortals
Look to it. As if reading
A scripture, men imitate infinity
And riches. Well, is the simple
Sky rich? Silver clouds are in fact
Like flowers. Yet rain down
Dew and damp. But when the simple
Blue is effaced, the sky,
Mat as marble, shines like ore,
Indicating riches.

[Was ist Gott . . .]

Was ist Gott? unbekannt, dennoch
Voll Eigenschaften ist das Angesicht
Des Himmels von ihm. Die Blize nemlich
Der Zorn sind eines Gottes. Jemehr ist eins
Unsichtbar,   schiket es sich in Fremdes. Aber der Donner
Der Ruhm ist Gottes. Die Liebe zur Unsterblichkeit
Das Eigentum auch, wie das unsere,
Ist eines Gottes.

[What is God . . .]

What is God? Unknown, yet
The face of the sky is filled
With his features. Lightning
Is the wrath of a god. The more invisible
This is,   befits the unfamiliar. But thunder
Is the glory of God. Love of immortality
Is also the property, like ours,
Of a god.

Fragments

Zu Sokrates Zeiten

Vormals richtete Gott.

Könige.

Weise.

wer richtet denn izt?

Richtet das einige
Volk? die heilge Gemeinde?
Nein! o nein! wer richtet denn izt?
ein Natterngeschlecht! feig und falsch
das edlere Wort nicht mehr
Über die Lippe
O im Nahmen
ruf ich
Alter Dämon! dich herab

Oder   sende
Einen Helden

Oder
die Weisheit.

In the Days of Socrates

Time was God judged.

            Kings.

        Sages.

              who judges now?

Is the entire people
   judge? the holy congregation?
   No! O No! who judges now?
           a race of vipers!   false and cowardly
               the nobler word no longer
      On the lips
O in the name of
                         I call you
       Down, old dæmon!

Or   send
   A hero

Or
   Wisdom

An

Elysium

Dort find ich ja

Zu euch ihr Todesgötter

Dort Diotima   Heroen.

Singen möcht ich von dir

Aber nur Thränen.

Und in der Nacht in der ich wandle erlöscht mir dein

Klares Auge!

himmlischer Geist.

To

Elysium

There I find

Toward you, O gods of death

There, Diotima   heroes.

Let me sing of you

                    But only tears.

And in the night wherein I wander, your clear eye

        Goes dead!

                        heavenly spirit.

An meine Schwester

Übernacht' ich im Dorf

Albluft

Straße hinunter

Haus Wiedersehn. Sonne der Heimath

Kahnfahrt,
Freunde   Männer und Mutter.
Schlummer.

Gestalt und Geist

Alles ist innig

  Das scheidet

So birgt der Dichter

Verwegner! möchtest von Angesicht zu Angesicht
  Die Seele sehn
        Du gehest in Flammen unter.

To My sister

I overnight in the village

Alp air

Down the lane

Home   reunion.   Native sun

Boating,
Friends   men and mother.
Slumber.

Shape and Spirit

Everything is inward

   This is the distinction

The poet thus conceals

Reckless! wanting to see the soul
   Face to face
            You go down in flames.

Sybille

Der Sturm
    Aber sie schmähn
        Schütteln gewaltig den Baum doch auch die
        thörigen Kinder werfen mit Steinen
die Äste beugt
    Und der Rabe singt
So wandert das Wetter Gottes über

Aber du heilger Gesang.

Und suchst armer Schiffer den gewohnten

Zu den Sternen siehe.

Der Baum

Da ich ein Kind, zag pflanzt ich dich

    Schöne Pflanze! wie sehn wir nun verändert uns
    Herrlich stehest   und

        wie ein Kind vor.

Sibyl

The storm
           But they hurl insults
                Shake the tree furiously even the silly children
                            throw stones
   branch bends
         And raven sings
God's weather passes over

   But you, holy song.

And poor sailor seeking the familiar

Look to the stars.

The Tree

A timid child, I planted you

    Lovely plant! how changed we see each other now
Splendid you stand   there

             like a child.

Aber die Sprache—
Im Gewitter spricht der
Gott.
Öfters hab' ich die Sprache
sie sagte der Zorn sei genug und gelte für den Apollo—
Hast du Liebe genug so zürn aus Liebe nur immer,
Öfters hab ich Gesang versucht, aber sie hörten dich nicht. Denn
so wollte die heilige Natur. Du sangest du für sie in deiner
　　　Jugend
nicht singend
Du sprachest zur Gottheit,
aber diß habt ihr all vergessen, daß immer die Erstlinge
　　　Sterblichen
nicht, daß sie den Göttern gehören.
gemeiner muß alltäglicher muß
die Frucht erst werden, dann wird
sie den Sterblichen eigen.

Im Walde

Du edles Wild.
Aber in Hütten wohnet der Mensch, und hüllet sich ein ins
verschämte Gewand, denn inniger ist achtsamer auch und
daß er bewahre den Geist, wie die Priesterin die himmlische
Flamme, diß ist sein Verstand. Und darum ist die Willkür
ihm und höhere Macht zu fehlen und zu vollbringen dem
Götterähnlichen, der Güter Gefährlichstes, die Sprache dem
Menschen gegeben, damit er schaffend, zerstörend, und
untergehend, und wiederkehrend zur ewiglebenden, zur
Meisterin und Mutter, damit er zeuge, was er sei geerbet zu
haben, gelernt von ihr, ihr Göttlichstes, die allerhaltende
Liebe.

But speech—
Thunderstorms are God
speaking.
I have often   speech
it said anger was enough and fit for Apollo—
Have you love enough, then simply let your anger rise from love,
I have often attempted song, but they did not hear you. This
was what holy Nature wished. You sang for them in your youth
no singer
you spoke to the deity,
but you have all forgotten that the first fruits belong
not to mortals, but to the gods.
more common, more daily a thing
must the fruit become, before
it pertain to mortals.

In the Forest

Noble deer.
But man lives in huts, wrapped in the garments of his
shame, and is the more inward, the more alert for it, and
that he tend his spirit as the priestess tends the heavenly
flame, this is his understanding. Which is why recklessness
and the higher power to fail and achieve are given him,
godlike creature, and language, most dangerous of
possessions, is given man so that creating, destroying,
perishing and returning back to her, eternal mistress and
mother, so that he might bear witness to what he is, having
inherited and learned from her the godliest of her attributes,
all-preserving love.

Denn nirgend bleibt er.
Es fesselt
Kein Zeichen.
Nicht immer

Ein Gefäß ihn zu fassen.

Denn gute Dinge sind drei.

Nicht will ich
Die Bilder dir stürmen.

      und das Sakrament
Heilig behalten, das hält unsre Seele
Zusammen, die uns gönnet Gott, das Lebenslicht
Das gesellige
Bis an unser End

He remains nowhere.
No sign
Binds.
Rarely

A vessel to grasp him.

Good things are three.

I have no wish
To destroy your images.

                   and maintaining the sacrament
Holy keeps our soul
Together, granted by God, life-light
Companion
To our end

Ein anderes freilich ists,

      Unterschiedenes ist
gut. Ein jeder
         und es hat
Ein jeder das Seine.

        dem dunklen Blatte,
     Und es war
Das Wachstum vernehmlich
    und   der syrische Boden,
   zerschmettert, und Flammen gleich unter den Sohlen
Es stach
Und der Ekel mich
Ankömt vom wütenden Hunger
Friedrich mit der gebißnen Wange
Eisenach
Die ruhmvollen

Barbarossa
Der Conradin

Ugolino—

Eugen
Himmelsleiter

     Der Abschied der Zeit
      und es scheiden im Frieden voneinander

It's something else to be sure,

                    Distinctions are
          good.   Each
                              and every
Has its own.

                              the dark leaf
                    And the growth
Was perceptible
          and   the Syrian soil
     shattered, and flames underfoot
Stinging
And queasiness coming
Over me from raving hunger
Friedrich with his bitten cheek
Eisenach
The renowned

Barbarossa
Conradin

Ugolino—

Eugenius
Jacob's ladder

          The farewell of Time
                    and in peace they part

So Mahomed, †Rinald,
Barbarossa, als freier Geist,

Kaiser Heinrich.
Wir bringen aber die Zeiten
untereinander
                Demetrius Poliorcetes
Peter der Große
                Heinrichs
Alpenübergang und daß
die Leute mit eigner Hand er gespeiset
und getränket und sein Sohn Konrad an Gift starb
Muster eines Zeitveränderers
Reformators
Conradin u. s. w.

alle, als Verhältnisse
bezeichnend.

†Höret das Horn des Wächters bei Nacht
  Nach Mitternacht ists um die fünfte Stunde

Thus Mohammed, † Rinaldo,
Barbarossa, qua free spirit

Emperor Heinrich.
But we confuse
our dates
          Demetrius Poliorcetes
Peter the Great
           Heinrich's
Crossing of the Alps and that
with his own hands he gave the people
food and drink and his son Conrad died of poison
Model of an innovator
reformer
Conradin, etc.

all significant
as relations.

†Hear the watchman's horn at night
  After midnight about the fifth hour

Tende   Strömfeld   Simonetta.
Teufen   Amyklä   Aveiro am Flusse
Fouga   die Familie   Alencastro den
Nahmen davon   Amalasuntha Antegon
Anathem Ardinghellus Sorbonne Cölestin
und Inozentius haben die Rede unter-
brochen und sie genannt den Pflanz-
garten der Französischen Bischöffe—
Aloisia Sigea *differentia vitae*
urbanae et rusticae Thermodon
ein Fluß in Cappadocien Val-
telino Schönberg Scotus Schönberg Teneriffa

Sulaco   Venafro
          Gegend
des Olympos.   Weißbrun in Nieder-
ungarn.   Zamora   Jacca   Baccho
Imperiali.   Genua   Larissa in Syrien

Wenn über dem Weinberg es flammt
Und schwarz wie Kohlen
Aussiehet um die Zeit
Des Herbstes der Weinberg, weil
Die Röhren des Lebens feuriger athmen
In den Schatten des Weinstoks. Aber
Schön ists, die Seele
Zu entfalten und das kurze Leben

Tende   Strömfeld   Simonetta.
Teufen   Amyclae   Aveiro on the river
Vouga   the family   Alencstro its
name therefrom   Amalasuntha Antegon
Anathem Ardinghellus Sorbonne Celestine
and Innocent interrupted the dis-
quisition and dubbed it (the Sorbonne)
the nursery of French bishops—
Aloisia Sigea *differentia vitae*
urbanae et rusticae Thermodon
a river in Cappadocia Val-
telino Schönberg Scotus Schönberg Tenerife

Sulaco   Venafro
              Region
of Olympos.   Weissbrunn in Lower
Hungary. Zamora   Jacca   Baccho
Imperiali.   Genoa   Larissa in Syria

When there are flames above the vineyard
Which looks coal-
Black around the time
Of autumn, since
The stalks of life breathe more fiery
In the shadows of the vine. But
It is a beautiful thing to unfold
The soul and this brief life

Und der Himmel wird wie eines Mahlers Haus
Wenn seine Gemählde sind aufgestellet.

Bei Thebe und Tiresias!
Mir will der Boden zu kahl seyn.

Ähnlich dem Manne, der Menschen frisset
Ist einer, der lebt ohne
(Liebe)

          und Schatten beschreibend hätt er
Der Augen Zorn

          Schlechthin
          diesesmal, oft aber
Geschiehet etwas um die Schläfe, nicht ist
Es zu verstehen, wenn aber eines Weges
Ein Freier herausgeht, findet
Daselbst es bereitet.

And the sky turns into a painter's house
With all his canvases on display.

Near Thebes and Tiresias!
The ground too bare for me.

Like the man who devours men
Is he who lives without
(Love)

and describing shadows, his eyes
Would fly into a rage

Quite plainly
this time, but often
Something happens around the temples, impossible
To understand this, but when a free man
Ventures out on a path, he finds it waiting
Right there.

Zu Rossen, ewige Lust
Zu Leben, wie wenn Nachtigallen
Süßen Ton der Heimath oder die Schneegans
Den Ton anstimmet über
Dem Erdkreis, sehnend,

                Streifen blauer Lilien
Kennest du   der Arbeit
Von Künstlern allein oder gleich
Dem Hirsch, der schweifet in der Hizze. Nicht
Ohn' Einschränkung.

Narcyssen Ranunklen und
Siringen aus Persien
Blumen Nelken, gezogen perlenfarb
Und schwarz und Hyacinthen,
Wie wemm es riechet, statt Musik
Des Eingangs, dort, wo böse Gedanken,
Liebende mein Sohn vergessen sollen einzugehen
Verhältnisse und diß Leben
Christophori   der Drache vergleicht der Natur
Gang und Geist und Gestalt.

Mare in heat, endless ache
For life, as when nightingales
Sing home's sweet tune, or the snow goose
Sets the tone, high above
The globe, longing,

                                    stripes of blue lilies
Do you know   of the work
Of artists alone or like
The stag rambling in the heat. Not
Without limitations.

Narcissi, ranunculi and
Syringas from Persia,
Flowers, carnations, cultivated in pearl
And black, and hyacinths,
As when the scent, instead of entrance
Music, is there, where evil thoughts,
My son, should forget to penetrate
Loving relations and this life
Of Christopher   the dragon like nature's
Movement mind and manner

Da soll er alles
Hinausführen
Außer den Langen
An eine reine Stätte
Da man die Asche
Hinschüttet, und solls
Verbrennen auf dem Holz mit Feuer.

Heidnisches
Jo Bacche, daß sie lernen der Hände Geschik
Samt selbigem,
Gerächet oder vorwärts. Die Rache gehe
Nemlich zurük. Und daß uns nicht
Dieweil wir roh sind,
Mit Wasserwellen Gott
                    Schlage. Nemlich
Gottlosen auch
Wir aber sind
Gemeinen gleich,
Die, gleich
Edeln Gott versuchet, ein Verbot
Ist aber, deß sich rühmen. Ein Herz sieht aber
Helden. Mein ist
Die Rede vom Vaterland. Das neide
Mir keiner. Auch so machet
Das Recht des Zimmermannes
Das Kreuz.

He should take
Everything
Except the long ones
To a clearing
Where ashes
Are scattered, and
Burn it on logs with fire.

From pagan
Io Bacche, let them learn skill of hand
And with selfsame, move
Forward or avenged. Vengeance, in fact, should
Reach back. And let God not
Lash us with waves
While we are
            raw. Indeed
Godless
We are
Like commoners
Whom God
Tempts like nobles, yet there is a law
Against glorying in this. But a heart sees
Heroes. Mine
To speak of my country. Let no one
Begrudge me that. By the same right
A carpenter makes
A cross.

Schwerdt
und heimlich Messer, wenn einer
geschliffen
            mittelmäßig Gut,
Daß aber uns das Vaterland nicht werde
Zum kleinen Raum. Schwer ist der
Zu liegen, mit Füßen, den Händen auch.
Nur Luft.

spizbübisch schnakisch
   Lächeln, wenn dem Menschen
seine kühnsten Hofnungen
   erfüllt werden

                    Sword
and concealed knife, when
        sharpened
                    halfway well,
But let our country not strike us
As too small a space. Heavy is the
To stretch out, with our feet, and hands too.
Just air.

rascally comic
        chortle when a man's
boldest hopes come true

Bauen möcht

und neu errichten
des Theseus Tempel und die Stadien
und wo Perikles gewohnet

Es fehlet aber das Geld, denn zu viel
ist ausgegeben heute. Zu Gaste nemlich hatt
ich geladen   und wir saßen beieinander

I want to build

and raise new
the temples of Theseus and the stadiums
and where Perikles lived

But there's no money, too much spent
today. I had a guest
over   and we sat together

In Lovely Blue

[In lieblicher Bläue . . .]

In lieblicher Bläue blühet mit dem metallenen Dache der
Kirchthurm. Den umschwebet Geschrei der Schwalben, den
umgiebt die rührendste Bläue. Die Sonne gehet hoch
darüber und färbet das Blech, im Winde aber oben stille
krähet die Fahne. Wenn einer unter der Gloke dann
herabgeht, jene Treppen, ein stilles Leben ist es, weil, wenn
abgesondert so sehr die Gestalt ist, die Bildsamkeit
herauskommt dann des Menschen. Die Fenster, daraus die
Gloken tönen, sind wie Thore an Schönheit. Nemlich, weil
noch der Natur nach sind die Thore, haben diese die
Ähnlichkeit von Bäumen des Walds. Reinheit aber ist auch
Schönheit. Innen aus Verschiedenem entsteht ein ernster
Geist. So sehr einfältig aber die Bilder, so sehr heilig sind
die, daß man wirklich oft fürchtet, die zu beschreiben. Die
Himmlischen aber, die immer gut sind, alles zumal, wie
Reiche, haben diese, Tugend und Freude. Der Mensch darf
das nachahmen. Darf, wenn lauter Mühe das Leben, ein
Mensch aufschauen und sagen: so will ich auch seyn? Ja. So
lange die Freundlichkeit noch am Herzen, die Reine, dauert,
misset nicht unglüklich der Mensch sich mit der Gottheit. Ist
unbekannt Gott? Ist er offenbar wie der Himmel? dieses
glaub' ich eher. Des Menschen Maaß ist's. Voll Verdienst,
doch dichterisch, wohnet der Mensch auf dieser Erde. Doch
reiner ist nicht der Schatten der Nacht mit den Sternen,
wenn ich so sagen könnte, als der Mensch, der heißet ein
Bild der Gottheit.

[In lovely blue . . .]

In lovely blue the steeple blossoms
With its metal roof. Around which
Drift swallow cries, around which
Lies most loving blue. The sun,
High overhead, tints the roof tin,
But up in the wind, silent,
The weathercock crows. When someone
Takes the stairs down from the belfry,
It is a still life, with the figure
Thus detached, the sculpted shape
Of man comes forth. The windows
The bells ring through
Are as gates to beauty. Because gates
Still take after nature,
They resemble the forest trees.
But purity is also beauty.
A grave spirit arises from within,
Out of divers things. Yet so simple
These images, so very holy,
One fears to describe them. But the gods,
Ever kind in all things,
Are rich in virtue and joy.
Which man may imitate.
May a man look up
From the utter hardship of his life
And say: Let me also be
Like these? Yes. As long as kindness lasts,
Pure, within his heart, he may gladly measure himself
Against the divine. Is God unknown?
Is he manifest as the sky? This I tend
To believe. Such is man's measure.
Well deserving, yet poetically
Man dwells on this earth. But the shadow
Of the starry night is no more pure, if I may say so,
Than man, said to be the image of God.

Giebt es auf Erden ein Maaß? Es giebt keines. Nemlich es
hemmen den Donnergang nie die Welten des Schöpfers.
Auch eine Blume ist schön, weil sie blühet unter der Sonne.
Es findet das Aug' oft im Leben Wesen, die viel schöner
noch zu nennen wären als die Blumen. O! ich weiß das
wohl! Denn zu bluten an Gestalt und Herz, und ganz nicht
mehr zu seyn, gefällt das Gott? Die Seele aber, wie ich
glaube, muß rein bleiben, sonst reicht an das Mächtige auf
Fittigen der Adler mit lobendem Gesange und der Stimme
so vieler Vögel. Es ist die Wesenheit, die Gestalt ist's. Du
schönes Bächlein, du scheinest rührend, indem du rollest so
klar, wie das Auge der Gottheit, durch die Milchstraße. Ich
kenne dich wohl, aber Thränen quillen aus dem Auge. Ein
heiteres Leben seh' ich in den Gestalten mich umblühen der
Schöpfung, weil ich es nicht unbillig vergleiche den
einsamen Tauben auf dem Kirchhof. Das Lachen aber
scheint mich zu grämen der Menschen, nemlich ich hab' ein
Herz. Möcht' ich ein Komet seyn? Ich glaube. Denn sie
haben die Schnelligkeit der Vögel; sie blühen an Feuer, und
sind wie Kinder an Reinheit. Größeres zu wünschen, kann
nicht des Menschen Natur sich vermessen. Der Tugend
Heiterkeit verdient auch gelobt zu werden vom ernsten
Geiste, der zwischen den drei Säulen wehet des Gartens.
Eine schöne Jungfrau muß das Haupt umkränzen mit
Myrthenblumen, weil die einfach ist ihrem Wesen nach und
ihrem Gefühl. Myrthen aber giebt es in Griechenland.

Is there measure on earth? There is
None. No created world ever hindered
The course of thunder. A flower
Is likewise lovely, blooming as it does
Under the sun. The eye often discovers
Creatures in life it would be yet lovelier
To name than flowers. O, this I know!
For to bleed both in body and heart, and cease
To be whole, is this pleasing to God?
But the soul, I believe, must
Remain pure, lest the eagle wing
Its way up to the Almighty with songs
Of praise and the voice of so many birds.
It is substance, and is form.
Lovely little brook, how moving you seem
As you roll so clear, like the eye of God,
Through the Milky Way. I know you well,
But tears pour from the eye.
I see gaiety of life blossom
About me in all creation's forms,
I do not compare it cheaply
To the graveyard's solitary doves. People's
Laughter seems to grieve me,
After all, I have a heart.
Would I like to be a comet? I think so.
They are swift as birds, they flower
With fire, childlike in purity. To desire
More than this is beyond human measure.
The gaiety of virtue also deserves praise
From the grave spirit adrift
Between the garden's three columns.
A beautiful virgin should wreathe her hair
With myrtle, being simple by nature and heart.
But myrtles are found in Greece.

Wenn einer in den Spiegel siehet, ein Mann, und siehet
darinn sein Bild, wie abgemahlt; es gleicht dem Manne.
Augen hat des Menschen Bild, hingegen Licht der Mond.
Der König Oedipus hat ein Auge zuviel vieleicht. Diese
Leiden dieses Mannes, sie scheinen unbeschreiblich,
unaussprechlich, unausdrüklich. Wenn das Schauspiel ein
solches darstellt, kommt's daher. Wie ist mir's aber, gedenk'
ich deiner jezt? Wie Bäche reißt das Ende von Etwas mich
dahin, welches sich wie Asien ausdehnet. Natürlich dieses
Leiden, das hat Oedipus. Natürlich ist's darum. Hat auch
Herkules gelitten? Wohl. Die Dioskuren in ihrer
Freundschaft haben die nicht Leiden auch getragen?
Nemlich wie Herkules mit Gott zu streiten, das ist Leiden.
Und die Unsterblichkeit im Neide dieses Lebens, diese zu
theilen, ist ein Leiden auch. Doch das ist auch ein Leiden,
wenn mit Sommerfleken ist bedekt ein Mensch, mit
manchen Fleken ganz überdekt zu seyn! Das thut die schöne
Sonne: nemlich die ziehet alles auf. Die Jünglinge führt die
Bahn sie mit Reizen ihrer Stralen wie mit Rosen. Die
Leiden scheinen so, die Oedipus getragen, als wie ein armer
Mann klagt, daß ihm etwas fehle. Sohn Laios, armer
Fremdling in Griechenland! Leben ist Tod, und Tod ist auch
ein Leben.

If a man look into a mirror
And see his image therein, as if painted,
It is his likeness. Man's image has eyes,
But the moon has light.
King Oedipus may have an eye too many.
The sufferings of this man seem indescribable,
Inexpressible, unspeakable. Which comes
When drama represents such things.
But what do I feel, now thinking of you?
Like brooks, I am carried away by the end of something
That expands like Asia. Of course,
Oedipus suffers the same? For a reason,
Of course. Did Hercules suffer as well?
Indeed. In their friendship
Did not the Dioscuri also suffer?
Yes, to battle God as Hercules did
Is to suffer. And to half share immortality
With the envy of this life,
This too is pain. But this also
Is suffering, when a man is covered with summer freckles,
All bespattered with spots. This is the work
Of the sun, it draws everything out.
It leads young men along their course,
Charmed by rays like roses.
The sufferings of Oedipus seem like a poor man
Lamenting what he lacks.
Son of Laios, poor stranger in Greece.
Life is death, and death a life.

Notes to the Poems

THE FOLLOWING notes restrict themselves to such information as might be helpful to the reader who comes to Hölderlin more or less from scratch. The incursions of commentary, paraphrase, and gloss are merely meant to graph possible areas of meaning: to encourage, not supplant, the reader's own invention.

In preparing these notes I have drawn on the commentaries provided in Beissner's *Grosse Stuttgarter Ausgabe* (1951), as well as the annotations included in the Beissner/Schmidt Insel Edition (1969), Mieth's Hanser Edition (1970), Lüders' *Studienausgabe* (1970), and Sattler's *Frankfurter Ausgabe* (1975). Certain notes on the *Hymns* are also indebted to Richard Unger's *Hölderlin's Major Poetry* (Bloomington, 1975), one of the most useful commentaries available to English-speaking readers.

Wherever possible I have based my versions on the reading texts provided by Sattler's Frankfurt Edition; otherwise I have used the texts established by Beissner's *Grosse Stuttgarter Ausgabe*. I have usually followed Hölderlin's own spellings of Greek names, however inconsistent these may be. The biblical citations are taken from the Authorized Version. Most of the datings of the poems are conjectural.

Nightsongs

Probably written in late 1802 or 1803.

Hölderlin alludes to working on these *Nachtgesänge* in a letter of December 1803. Nine *Nightsongs*—six odes and the three short poems included here—were published in Friedrich Wilmans' *Taschenbuch für das Jahr 1805*. They were to be the last poems Hölderlin saw into print.

In Hölderlin's vocabulary the word "night" often signifies that state of spiritual numbness which follows upon the death of the gods. A locus of loss, a gap between days, night is a time for remembering, a time for waiting.

Half of Life / Hälfte des Lebens

Hölderlin was thirty-five the year this text was first published, *nel mezzo del cammin*. He wrote to his sister on December 11, 1800: "I cannot bear the idea that I, like so many others who find themselves at that critical point in life when a deadening anxiety, greater than anything known in youth, accumulates around our inner being, that I, merely in order to go on, must become so cold, so utterly sober, so closed off. In fact I often feel like ice, and feel this is necessary as long as I lack some quieter refuge, some place where those things which concern me would touch me less closely and hence cause me less commotion."

The Shelter at Hahrdt / Der Winkel von Hahrdt

Not far from Hölderlin's native Nürtingen, among the woods that overlook the Aich Valley near the village of Hardt, stands a natural shelter created by two large slabs of sandstone tilted against each other. The rock formation is known as the Ulrich Stone. According to local legend, it was here, in 1519, that Duke Ulrich of Württemberg managed to hide out from his enemy nobles among the Swabian League. A nearby rock is said to bear the trace of his footprint: a landscape inscribed with myth.

Ages of Life / Lebensalter

The topos is drawn from the celebrated description of Palmyra in the first chapter of Volney's *Les Ruines, ou méditations sur les révolutions des empires* (1791): "After three days travelling through an arid wilderness, having traversed the valley of caves and sepulchres, on issuing into the plain, I was suddenly struck with a scene of the most stupendous ruins— a countless multitude of superb columns, stretching in avenues beyond the reach of sight. Among them were magnificent edifices, some entire, others in ruins. The ground was covered on all sides with fragments of cornices, capitals, shafts, entablatures, pilasters, all of white marble, and of the most exquisite workmanship. ... Darkness now increased, and already, through the dusk, I could distinguish nothing more than the pale fantasies of columns and walls. The solitude of the place, the tranquillity of the hour, the majesty of the scene, impressed on my mind a religious pensiveness. The aspect of a great city deserted, the memory of times past, compared with its present state, all elevated my mind to high contemplations. I sat on the shaft of a column; and there, my elbow reposing on my knee, and head reclining on my hand, my eyes fixed, sometimes on the desert, sometimes on the ruins, I fell into a profound revery."

Hymns

The poems in this section, composed for the most part between 1801 and 1803, have traditionally been gathered by Hölderlin's various editors under the collective rubric of *Hymns*. The title is not Hölderlin's; the closest he comes to characterizing these texts is in the letter to Wilmans of December 1803, where he contrasts the "tired flight" of love songs with the "high and pure jubilation of patriotic songs" (*das hohe und reine Frohlocken vaterländischer Gesänge*). These hymns may therefore be understood as Hölderlin's attempt to move beyond the personal concerns of his earlier love lyrics, elegies, or odes into more public, more national songs of praise. As he notes in the dedication to his translation of *Antigone* (1804): "I wish to sing of the forefathers of our Prince, of their ancestral seats, and of the angels of our holy Fatherland." Since the word "Fatherland," in Hölderlin's language, has none of the unfortunate overtones it has since acquired, I have chosen to translate it throughout as "native land." These hymns, then, may be thought of as "native songs."

At the Source of the Danube / Am Quell der Donau

1801. The first two strophes of the poem are apparently missing; they would have filled out the triadic structure of the hymn: (12, 12), 15; 12, 12, 16; 12, 12, 14. Judging from the various drafts of the poem, the hymn was to have opened with an invocation to Mother Asia.

The easterly course of the Danube from Germany to the Black Sea is an image of the potential dialogue between Occident and Orient, between present and past. As the river's place of origin (the source of the Danube lies at Donaueschingen, on the eastern slopes of the Black Forest mountains), Hölderlin's Swabia thus stands in significant relation to Asia—source of the divine Word, home of patriarchs and prophets, cradle of humanity. Though the light of origins may be too blinding to sustain, the hymn suggests that some of the inaugural intensity of Greece or Asia may be recovered through the mediation of memory or nature. Most of the place names are drawn from Pindar. Cf. Wordsworth's "The Source of the Danube."

PAGE 55 *Parnassos*. Mountain above Delphi, sacred to Apollo and the muses.

    Kithairon. Mountain range near Thebes, associated with Dionysian rites.

    Capitol. Site of the temple of Jupiter in Rome.

PAGE 57 *Ionia*. Region along the western coast of Asia Minor, colonized by the Greeks.

    Isthmos. The Isthmus of Corinth, site of the Isthmian Games.

    Kephisos. Small river near Athens.

Taygetos. Mountain range overlooking the valley of Sparta.

Kaukasos. Mountain range between the Black and Caspian
  Seas.

Rooted on mountaintops days on end. Perhaps an allusion to
  Moses on Mount Sinai.

The Migration / Die Wanderung

Spring 1801. First published in 1802.

The boundaries evoked in the first strophe recall the dimensions of
the great medieval duchy of Swabia under the rule of the Hohenstaufer.
Until the thirteenth century Swabia stretched southward to include Ger-
man-speaking Switzerland; to the west it comprised southern Baden,
Württemberg, and Alsace, and to the east, the western portion of Ba-
varia.

Beissner suggests that the journey of the "German tribe" down the
Danube and their meeting with the "children of the sun" at the Black
Sea may allude to the Swabian settlers who emigrated toward the lower
basin of the Danube in 1770; on the other hand, Hölderlin may simply
be constructing a genealogical myth in the manner of Hesiod or Pindar.

PAGE 61   *Lombardy.* Region of northern Italy that borders on Switz-
          erland.

          Neckar. Major river in Swabia that flows through Tübingen,
          Nürtingen, and Stuttgart.

PAGE 63   *They call this sea Hospitable.* The Greek colonists termed
          the Black Sea πόντος εὔξεινος.

PAGE 65   *Cayster.* The Kaistrios, a river in Ionia.

          Taygetos. Mountain range overlooking the valley of Sparta.

          Hymettos. Mountain range southeast of Athens, known for
          its honey and marble.

          Tmolos. The river Paktolos, famed for its gold, runs down
          from Mount Tmolos in Lydia.

          Land of Homer. I.e., Ionia.

          The young peaches you sent to me. The peach (known in Latin
          as *malum persicum*, or Persian apple) was introduced to
          Europe from Asia Minor. The great Graeco-Asian culture
          of Ionia is another such fruit.

          Thetis. A sea nymph, daughter of the sea god Nereos and
          mother of Achilles.

          Ida. Mountain range to the south of Troy.

          One of her sons, the Rhine. The territory of the medieval
          duchy of Swabia included the source of the Rhine in

German Switzerland. See also the notes to the following
poem, "The Rhine."

PAGE 67   *Graces of Greece*. The Charites: Euphrosyne, Aglaia, and
Thalia. See Pindar's Fourteenth Olympian, translated by
Hölderlin.

The Rhine / Der Rhein

1801. First published in Seckendorf's *Musenalmanach für das Jahr 1808*.
One of the manuscripts of the poem contains the following marginal
note in Hölderlin's hand:

> The law of this song is that the first two parts, by their pro-
> gression and regression, are opposite in form but alike in con-
> tent; the two following parts are alike in form but opposite in
> content; but the final part balances everything out with a per-
> vasive metaphor.

This brief gloss only hints at the intricate architectonics of this hymn,
analyzed in depth by such commentators as Beissner, Böschenstein, and
Ryan.

The poem contains fifteen strophes, which are divided into five groups
of three. The first two triads of the poem (strophes 1–3, 4–6) are "alike
in content" since their primary subject is the course of the demigod
Rhine from birth to maturity. The two following triads are "opposite"
in content: strophes 7–9 no longer deal explicitly with the river but
rather with various aspects of Titanic excess; by contrast, Rousseau, the
subject of strophes 10–12, embodies a more exemplary (and more his-
torical) mode of heroism that consciously blends rebellion with affir-
mation, action with mediation. The "pervasive metaphor" of the final
part (strophes 13–15) involves the bridal feast celebrating the apocalyp-
tic marriage of mortals and gods.

As for the "form" of the component triads, Hölderlin's comment on
"progression and regression" seems to indicate that he is referring to
the directional movement of thought through the poem, or to what he
elsewhere terms the "rhythm of representation." Ryan and other com-
mentators have elucidated this dimension of the hymn through Höl-
derlin's theory of the *Wechsel der Töne*—the alternation or modulation
of tones. In his theoretical essays Hölderlin attempts to define and cor-
relate three essential tonalities of poetry: the *naive* (expression of the
sensibility; related to the lyric), the *heroic* (expression of activity; related
to the epic), and the *ideal* (expression of the intellect; related to the
drama). According to this scheme, the first strophe of "The Rhine" is

naive in tone, that is, serene and evocative; the second strophe, with its narrative of conflict, modulates into the *heroic* tone; while the third strophe is *ideal*, that is, reflective, moving from particulars into philosophic generality. The "progression" of tones in these first three strophes (*naive →heroic → ideal*) is reversed in the following triad (*ideal → heroic → naive*). The third and fourth triads of the poem (strophes 7–9 and 10–12) both proceed through an identical succession of tones (*heroic → ideal → naive*), all of which are "balanced out" or dialectically synthesized in the concluding section.

Isaak von Sinclair, to whom the poem is dedicated, was one of Hölderlin's most loyal friends. A sympathizer of the French Revolution and political activist who shared Hölderlin's dream of a Swabian Republic, Sinclair was expelled from the university of Jena in 1795 for his participation in student disturbances. In early 1805 Sinclair was arrested, tried, and held for four months on charges of high treason against the Grand Duke of Württemberg (see Introduction). Given the dedication to Sinclair certain scholars have been tempted to interpret the poem in markedly political terms. Bertaux, for example, notes that the Rhine is described in the hymn as "freeborn" in order to underscore its source in the republican soil of Switzerland. Rousseau, the hero of strophes 10–12, is equally associated with revolutionary prophecy, while the concluding lines of the poem, Bertaux argues, contain a veiled reference to the steel blade of the tyrannicide.

PAGE 71   *Ticino and Rhône.* These two rivers rise near the source of the Rhine in the Swiss Alps. The Rhine flows eastward from its source (hence is "driven towards Asia") before turning north toward Lake Constance. The initial course of the river thus parallels the southerly vector of the poet's thoughts in the first strophe as they drift toward Italy and Morea (i.e., the Peloponnesos).

A riddle, the pure of source. In German: *Ein Rätsel ist ein Reinentsprungenes.* This gnome contains a pun on *Rhein* (the river) and *rein* (pure). The syntax is also reversible: that which springs (or descends) from a pure source is a riddle; a riddle (or enigma) is a linguistic and ontological phenomenon that bespeaks pure origin.

PAGE 73   *And tears these snakes.* An allusion to the infant Hercules struggling with the snakes placed in his cradle by jealous Hera.

PAGE 77   *Rousseau.* A demigod, like the Rhine itself and the Promethean rebels evoked in the previous triad, Rousseau is here associated with the sacred excess and martyrdom of Dionysos. Hölderlin construes Rousseau as a prophet and poet whose destiny lies in the linguistic acts of naming and interpreting (*deuten*). He is not merely the Mosaic lawgiver of the French Revolution but rather a promulgator of language in its purest and holiest form.

Lake Bienne. Hounded by persecutors both real and imaginary, Rousseau took refuge in 1765 on the Ile St. Pierre in the Swiss Lake Bienne (or Bielersee): see Book 12 of his *Confessions.* The achieved serenity of this and the following strophe—a green thought in a green shade—interpret the text of the "Cinquième Promenade" of Rousseau's *Rêveries d'un promeneur solitaire.*

PAGE 81   *But a wise man managed to stay lucid.* Socrates at the conclusion of Plato's *Symposium* (or *Banquet*).

The Only One / Der Einzige

Probably drafted in the fall of 1802, around the same time as "Patmos." Two later versions of the poem exist, believed to have been written in 1803.

The "unique" or "only one" of the title is Christ. The poem attempts to situate Christ in relation to the Hellenic pantheon: Is he distinct from all previous gods of antiquity (as Christian dogma would have it), or is he in fact their final and most perfect descendant, the "jewel" of their house? The hymn vacillates between the poet's intellectual intuition of the unity behind all manifestations of the divine and his emotional inability to reconcile his excessive dependence on salvation through Christ with a broader, more inclusive vision of the gods.

PAGE 83   *Elis.* The region in the western Peloponnesos where
               Olympia lies.
            Smyrna . . . Ephesos. Greek settlements in Ionia, on the
               western coast of Asia Minor.
PAGE 85   *My master and Lord.* Christ. Cf. John 13:13.
            the brother/Of Euios. Euios was one of the cult names of
               Dionysos. The latter plays an important role in Hölderlin's work: in "Brot und Wein" (where he is also juxtaposed with Christ) Dionysos comforts men with quiet joy, allowing them to endure the night that has fallen in the absence of the gods; in "Dichterberuf" he awakens the nations from their spiritual apathy; here, brother to

Herakles, Dionysos bears civilization from India to the West, for by taming the tygers of wrath and by founding vineyards, he effects the transformation of nature into culture. Yet despite this insight into their fraternity, the poet in the next strophe shies from fully equating these demigods (or "worldly men") with Christ: though a "captive" on earth like Herakles and Dionysos (and the poet himself), Christ remains singular, unique.

Patmos

1802. First published in Seckendorf's *Musenalmanach* in 1808.

"Patmos" was presented (by Sinclair) to the Landgrave Friedrich of Hessen–Homburg in January 1803, on the occasion of the latter's fifty-fifth birthday. The landgrave was a conservative defender of Christian law and order who had written several pamphlets condemning Enlightenment impiety and Jacobin libertarianism. In 1802, distressed by the political and intellectual upheavals incited by the French Revolution, he commissioned Klopstock to write a poem in defense of traditional biblical values, but since the elderly poet was unable to fulfill the request, Hölderlin took on the task. The final two strophes of the hymn, recommending reverent study of Holy Scripture, may be directly addressed to the pious landgrave. The poem abounds in biblical allusions, most of them drawn from the Gospel According to St. John. Following contemporary assumption, Hölderlin conflates John of Patmos, author of the Apocalypse, and the apostle John into a single seer who witnesses the end of an eon and foretells the Second Coming. A later version of the poem (see p. 103) superimposes yet another prophetic John—the beheaded Baptist. Over the course of the hymn the "I" of the poet and the composite figure of John blend into a single shared memory (and anticipation) of Christ.

PAGE 89   *Near and/Hard to grasp. Nah ist/Und schwer zu fassen der Gott./Wo aber Gefahr ist, wächst/Das Rettende auch.* A celebrated crux: Does the danger consist in the very nearness of the divine, or does the peril rather lie in the difficulty of grasping it?
   A genius. Cf. Ezekiel 8:3, "And he put forth the form of an hand, and took me by a lock of mine head; and the spirit lifted me up between the earth and the heaven, and brought me in the visions of God to Jerusalem." One might also juxtapose Chapter 4 of Volney's *Les Ruines* (see p. 256) in which the author tells how, in the

course of his meditations on ruins, he was seized by the Genius of Liberty and transported into the heavens: "Suddenly a celestial flame seemed to dissolve the bands which fix us to the earth, and like a light vapor, borne up on the wings of the Genius, I felt myself wafted to the regions above. Thence, from the aerial heights, looking down on the earth, I beheld a scene entirely new. Under my feet, floating in the void, a globe, like that of the moon, but smaller and less luminous, presented to me one of its phases."

PAGE 91   *Asia.* I.e., Ionia, Tmolus, Taurus, and Messogis are all mountains in Asia Minor.

Patmos. Located in the Aegean archipelago, the island of Patmos occupies a privileged space between the Hellenic and Judeo-Christian worlds, for it was here that John the Divine wrote the Apocalypse. The ascetic darkness and poverty of the island offer a place of refuge and meditation, while its scorched landscape echoes the poet's own spiritual devastation. Cf. Revelation 1:9, "I John, who also am your brother, and companion in tribulation, and in the kingdom and patience of Jesus Christ, was in the isle that is called Patmos, for the word of God, and for the testimony of Jesus Christ."

PAGE 93   *The storm-bearer.* This epithet, sometimes associated with Dionysos, is here applied to Christ. His Dionysian attributes are further emphasized by the allusion to the "mystery of the vine" several lines later. Cf. John 15:5, "I am the vine, ye are the branches." As in Hölderlin's "Brot und Wein" the rites of bread and wine can equally refer to the liturgies of Dionysos or to the Christian Eucharist. Like Dionysos, Christ must first die and be dismembered before he can be reborn and regathered into future remembrance.

The banquet hour. The banquet in Plato's *Symposium* is here rhymed with the Last Supper: both are love-feasts. Cf. John 15:12–13, "This is my commandment, That ye love one another, as I have loved you. Greater love hath no man than this, that a man lay down his life for his friends."

Evening had come. The close of the ancient Day of divine presence, consummated with the death of Christ. The first several lines of this strophe appear to allude to the apparition of Christ at Emmaus. Cf. Luke 24:14–17, "And they talked together of all these things which had happened. And it came to pass, that, while they communed together and reasoned, Jesus himself drew near, and went with them. But their eyes were holden that they should not know him. And he said unto them, What manner of communications are these that ye have one to another, as ye walk, and are sad?"

PAGE 95 *He sent them/The Spirit.* Cf. Acts 2:1–4, "And when the day of Pentecost was fully come, they were all with one accord in one place. And suddenly there came a sound from heaven as of a rushing mighty wind, and it filled all the house where they were sitting. And there appeared unto them cloven tongues like as of fire, and it sat upon each of them. And they were all filled with the Holy Ghost, and began to speak with other tongues, as the Spirit gave them utterance."

the kingly sun's/Light went out. Another reference to the extinction of the divine light at the death of the solar god, Christ. The night of the ensuing historical age must endure his absence: until Parousia he will be accessible only as mediate memory or image.

PAGE 97 *Calling Evil by its name.* To be contrasted with Christ's last words in the sixth strophe: "All is Good." If Good is the highest manifestation of God, then Evil may be understood as distance from the divine, as an agony of dispersion and fragmentation.

the winnower scooping wheat. These lines conflate the parable of the sower in Mark 4:3–9 and the prophecy of John the Baptist recounted in Matthew 3:11–12, " . . . he that cometh after me is mightier than I, whose shoes I am not worthy to bear: he shall baptize you with the Holy Ghost, and with fire: Whose fan is in his hand, and he will throughly purge his floor, and gather his wheat into the garner; but he will burn up the chaff with unquenchable fire."

To shape an image of him. These and the following lines allude to the dangers of iconolatry, of violating the divine through presumptuous imitation and representation. God must remain a sign: to be read or figuratively interpreted but not to be copied.

PAGE 99   *A sign of deliverance.* The name of Christ will be a *Losungs-zeichen* or "pass-sign" which, after the triumphal march of history has reached its zenith, will enable the gods to (re)descend upon the earth. Yet the following lines again evoke the perils of direct contact with the divine fire as opposed to the gentler, more intermediary radiance of Holy Scripture.

PAGE 101   *His sign/Is silent.* The visible sign of God is the lightning bolt, now silent because the time for direct revelation of the divine is no longer and not yet at hand. During this intervening period of darkness, the active memory of Christ may permit interpretation of the divine design of history.

Patmos / [Fragments of a later version]

Said to date from the summer or fall of 1803.

PAGE 103   *From Jordan.* Cf. the accounts of Christ's miracle working in Matthew 5:23–25 and John 4:43–54.
            I shall tarry a while. John 13:33, "Little children, yet a little while I am with you."
            the head/Of the Baptist. Cf. Matthew 14:8–11 and Mark 6:25–28.
            Hercules. For the brotherhood of Hercules and Christ, see "The Only One."
            Peleus. Father of Achilles, shipwrecked on the island of Kos, not far from Patmos.
            A fate rings differently. I.e., Christ's fate.
            the knights. I.e., the Crusaders.
            Heinrich . . . at Canossa. The German Emperor Heinrich IV did three days of penance at Canossa in 1077 in order to absolve himself from excommunication by Pope Gregory VII.

PAGE 105   *dragon's teeth.* Just as the Spartoi sprung from the dragon's teeth sowed by Kadmos on the Theban plain, so the Holy Spirit at Pentecost makes constructive, eloquent heroes out of the grieving disciples.

Remembrance / Andenken

First published in Seckendorf's *Musenalmanach* in 1808. Generally believed to have been composed in the spring of 1803, though Sattler has recently argued that it should be dated as late as 1805. A draft of the final strophe of *Andenken* appears on the manuscript containing *Der Ister*, and both poems may be read as extensions of the riverine meditations of the earlier Danube and Rhine hymns. As its title indicates, *Andenken* is suffused with recollections of Hölderlin's ill-fated journey to Bordeaux. Heidegger, however, interprets this An-Denken ("thinking of," "thinking toward," "thinking in relation to") as fundamental to poetic thinking or dwelling in general. His line-by-line commentary on the poem may be found in his *Erläuterungen zu Hölderlins Dichtung*.

PAGE 107   *The northeasterly*. The wind, directly addressed in the fifth line, blows from northeast to southwest, from the poet's native Germany to (remembered) Bordeaux. The fire (or more literally, "the fiery spirit") that it promises to seafarers (and poets) is perhaps the "fire of heaven" of which Hölderlin speaks in letters to Böhlendorff: the experience of its devastating alterity enables recognition (and remembrance) of the way back home.

     A fragrant cupful/Of dark light. Possibly a reference to the rich bouquet and luminous body of Bordeaux red wine.

PAGE 109   *Bellarmin*. The friend to whom the hero of Hölderlin's epistolary novel, *Hyperion*, addresses his letters.

     There are those/Who shy from the source. The subject would seem to be the "friends" of the preceding line or the "sailors" of the first strophe. In their hesitation to go or return to the source ("an die Quelle zu gehn"), they are like rivers whose course leads seaward, away from their origin. Yet it is only in the sea, in the solitary and arduous process of voyaging far from the familiar, that the source may be recalled: oblivion is integral to memory.

     To the Indies. The manuscript version of this strophe reads *Indien* (i.e., India), while the printed text reads *Indiern* (i.e., Indians). I have translated this as "Indies" in order to retain that fortunate confusion of East and West historically associated with the term.

     From that breezy spit of land. Possibly the Bec d'Ambès, a narrow tongue of land at the confluence of the river Garonne and Dordogne just beyond Bordeaux.

     But poets establish what remains. In German: *Was bleibet aber, stiften die Dichter*. The verb *stiften* translates into a variety of actions: to found, inaugurate, originate, institute, donate, bring about, etc.

The Ister / Der Ister

Summer 1803? 1805? The Ister (Istros) is the ancient Greek name for the Danube. See the notes to "At the Source of the Danube."

PAGE 111   *Indus/And Alpheus.* Two rivers associated with origins; the Alpheus runs by Olympia.

Adequacy to fate. A periphrase for *das Schickliche,* a term dense with implications. The adjective *schicklich* literally means "proper," "appropriate," "fit," "decent." Hölderlin's nominalized form of the adjective also contains resonances of the verb *sich schicken* ("to conform to," "submit to"), as well as echoes of *Geschick* or *Schicksal* ("destiny," "fate") and *geschickt* ("adept," "skilled"). The entire semantic cluster alludes to the capacity to achieve an apt and decorous relation to what is meted out by fate, the ability to maintain skill in measure. The notion of adequacy (etymologically, "equalize") seemed to best include these dimensions.

Hercules. Pindar's Third Olympian (translated by Hölderlin) recounts Hercules' journey to the source of the Danube in the land of the Hyperboreans. It was from this region that he brought back the olive trees that he planted around the unshaded Olympic fields; the olive branch subsequently became a symbol of Olympic victory. Hercules is thus a heroic mediator of that dialectic between Hellenic fire and Hesperidean shadow which Hölderlin outlines in his letter to Böhlendorff of December 4, 1801 (see Introduction).

PAGE 113   *The Rhine, ran off/Sideways.* Reference to the lateral easterly course of the Rhine at its source.

All that is needed/Is a sign. Rivers at once divide and unify wet and dry, nature and culture, sky and earth, gods and mortals. As signs they make the divine process manifest, allowing it to descend to earth, or into language.

Hertha. Ancient Germanic goddess of fertility, Mother Earth.

this one here . . . all too placid. The Danube, whose infant course through Swabia is in marked contrast to the more mature majesty of the Rhine.

Mnemosyne

Fall 1803? There are a number of variant manuscript versions of this hymn, and scholars differ in their establishment of the text, particularly regarding the first strophe (see p. 277). I follow the reading provided in the *Einleitung* to the new *Frankfurter Ausgabe* of Hölderlin's works edited by D. E. Sattler, who dates this poem as late as summer of 1805. According to Beissner, the manuscripts indicate that the lines at the outset of the third strophe—"By the figtree/My Achilles died"—were the kernel out of which the rest of the poem grew. Since Mnemosyne is the Greek goddess of memory and mother of the Muses, the title would seem to allude to the poet's anxious recollection of the dead, in particular the heroes of the *Iliad*.

PAGE 119 *My Achilles*. Hölderlin expresses this same personal attachment in his brief essay "On Achilles." "He is my favorite hero, at once strong and tender, the most perfect and most ephemeral flower of the heroic world."

Ajax. According to Beissner, Hölderlin's translations from Sophocles' *Ajax* are contemporary with the composition of this hymn. Particularly relevant is Hölderlin's version of the suicide speech in which Ajax, dying far from his native Salamis, bids farewell to nature—to the grottoes, the groves, and the streams around Troy (among which, the river Skamandros). The following lines of this strophe refer to the fit of madness (or divine possession) that brought on Ajax's suicide.

Patroklos. See Book 16 of the *Iliad*: Patroklos died in the armor that Achilles had loaned him. The juxtaposition of Ajax and Patroklos is all the more pointed here, given the fact that Ajax killed himself in anger, when, in the wake of Patroklos's death, he was not awarded the armor of Achilles. An earlier version of these lines more explicitly contrasts Ajax's fate—suicide and madness— with that of Achilles and Patroklos—heroic death in battle. Though they seem to differ considerably, both these destinies are the products of divine compulsion; man is not free to choose his fate:

> And many others
> Also died. Many by their own hand,
> Despondent, minds in disarray, under divine
> Compulsion to the bitter end; while others died
> On the field, standing under Fate.

Eleutherai. Hesiod's *Theogony* speaks of the goddess Mnemosyne as reigning "over the hills of Eleuther." Kithairon is a mountain range near Thebes.

to cut/Her lock of hair. In Euripides' *Alcestis* Death has a black garment, black wings, and a knife to cut off a lock of hair as an offering to the gods below. These lines speak of the darkness that fell at the close of the ancient Day of divine presence: When even Memory has died, how is poetry possible? Yet, as the final line of the hymn suggests, to grieve excessively for this loss is to risk the fate of Ajax.

Drafts of Hymns

Scholars generally concur in dating the poems grouped here between 1801 and 1806; they are arranged in what is presumed to be their chronological order. Following the example of Beissner's *Grosse Stuttgarter Ausgabe*, most of Hölderlin's editors have labeled these texts as *Hymnische Entwürfe*—sketches or drafts of hymns.

[As birds drift by . . .] / [Wie Vögel langsam ziehn . . .]

The central simile may derive from Deuteronomy 32:11–12, "As an eagle stirreth up her nest, fluttereth over her young, spreadeth abroad her wings, taketh them, beareth them on her wings: So the Lord alone did lead him, and there was no strange god with him." The "Prince" in the third line plays on the German etymology of the word *Fürst*: he is the "first" or "foremost" among the younger birds.

[Like seacoasts . . .] / [Wie Meeresküsten . . .]

Another extended simile: like the precious goods that came to Greece through sea trade, so Dionysos and Aphrodite bear ashore that wealth of inspiration and beauty upon which song is built.

To the Madonna / An die Madonna

Evidence suggests that this text is contemporary with Hölderlin's other great Christian hymns "The Only One" and "Patmos."

PAGE 133   *I have suffered much.* May refer to the poet's attempts to reconcile his strict Protestant upbringing with his reverence for the pagan gods.

the beauty/Of my homegrown speech. Lutheran German, as

against the Latin in which the Virgin Mary is traditionally addressed.

the lily. Emblem of the Virgin.

PAGE 135 *named John/By his mute father.* John the Baptist, son of Elisabeth and Zacharias. The latter was struck dumb for doubting the annunciation of the angel Gabriel, but upon the birth of his son, "they made signs to his father, how he would have him called. And he asked for a writing table, and wrote, saying, His name is John. And they marvelled all. And his mouth was opened immediately, and his tongue loosed, and he spake and praised God" (Luke 1:62–64). On the function of prophecy, interpretation, and naming, see the notes to "Patmos."

For laws are good. In his translation of Sophocles' Antigone Hölderlin employs the same word (*Satzungen*) for those "unwritten laws" that transcend Creon's civil statutes. The following lines of this strophe refer to King Herod, who had John the Baptist decapitated, and to the rabble responsible for the death of Christ.

PAGE 137 *give renewed growth.* In the times of darkness that follow upon the death of Christ and the ancient gods the Virgin Mary acts as an Earth Mother who oversees those organic processes which may eventually lead to the new (Hesperidean) dawn.

PAGE 139 *Never leaving their mother's/Lap.* Hölderlin writes to his brother (January 1, 1799): "I believe that the basic virtues and failings of the Germans can be reduced to their rather narrow-minded domesticity. They are everywhere *glebae addicti*, and most of them are stuck, literally or metaphorically, in their own clod of earth." For the "young race" provinciality is as great a danger as dispersion. Certain commentators see the "nurse" of the previous lines as Greece, midwife of the coming Hesperidean Day.

let the wilderness/Be spared. During the "holy night" that falls between the divine past and future, nature ceases to be a humanized garden and instead reverts to wilderness (*Wildniβ*). Though the term wilderness relates to Hölderlin's concept of "aorgic" energy (see Introduction, p. 18), it seems to be used in a more positive sense here, akin to that state of unorganized innocence (or Beulah) which Blake portrays in *The Book of Thel*.

Knochenberg. A mountain near Bad Driburg in Westphalia that Hölderlin visited with Heinse and Diotima in the summer of 1796. Its name (literally, "Bone Mountain") equates it with Ossa, a mountain in Thessaly associated with the struggle between the Giants and the Olympian gods. The allusion to Teutoburg evokes yet another site of battle, for it was in this region that the Romans fought the ancient Germans under Arminius. Beissner also hears echoes of Golgotha (etymologically derived from "skull") in this paronomastic landscape. The "spirited waters" mentioned further on are probably the mineral springs for which the Bad Driburg area is famous.

PAGE 143   *the god of victory, the liberator*. May be an ambiguous reference to Napoleon, the Titan prince whose armies were despoiling Mother Germany.

The Titans / Die Titanen

In Hölderlin's late work the Titans embody those chaotic, originating forces that precede the coming of the Olympians. Like Shelley's Demogorgon or Prometheus, the Titans are located at once *before* and *below*: they occupy a place of anteriority (and proximity) to the gods, while at the same time representing the unbounded, undisciplined rejection of divine order. The age of the Titans, Hölderlin thus intimates, resembles our own, a time of preparatory confusion.

PAGE 145   *holy wilderness*. As in "To the Madonna" the present is pictured as wilderness; within this wasteland, however, may lie the roots of an ultimate intensity. Cf. "The Argument" of Blake's *Marriage of Heaven and Hell*: "Roses are planted where thorns grow./And on the barren heath/Sing the honey bees."

PAGE 147   *But banquets/Give pleasure*. Consolations in a time of disarray: banquets, children playing, bees, birds.

   the lightning/Chains sparkle. God strikes as lightning, usually fatal. Here, however, the new Day slides down lightning rods like morning dew, imperceptibly assimilating itself into the rhythms of everyday activity.

PAGE 149   *For gross things must also enter/The balance*. The very gross-

ness of the Titans engenders the realization that some-
thing purer may be at hand.

And the mover and shaker. However the Titans may rage in
the lower depths when Father Zeus reaches down to
awaken mankind from its death, the subsequent strug-
gles between the chthonic powers of the underworld
and the Olympians only serve to fortify the coherence
of the coming gods. Cf. Keats's treatment of the dis-
placement of the Titans in *Hyperion.*

[I once asked the muse . . .] / [Einst hab ich die Muse gefragt . . .]

This and the following poem seem to be closely associated; Hellin-
grath suggests they are portions of a larger cycle dealing with the Titans.
Most commentators identify the Prince (*Fürst*) of line 20 with Hercules,
battling the unruly powers of the abyss in his Twelfth Labor.

[But when the gods . . .] / [Wenn aber die Himmlischen . . .]

This text is so elliptical that a tentative paraphrase might be risked.

PAGE 155   Out of the primal struggle between sky and earth, be-
tween the Thunderer and his daughter, the mountains
emerge, built by the ray of divine light. But as the
Thunderer descends upon the earth in demiurgic wrath
and joy, he runs the risk of losing sight of his heavenly
origin: wisdom must maintain an appropriate measure
between high and low, sky and earth, mountain and
lake, isle and ocean.

PAGE 157   Rampant "aorgic" growth (see Introduction, p. 18) is
merely a parody of divine creation; it tricks mortals into
mistaking the wilderness for a garden. Though Hölder-
lin sometimes uses the term "wilderness" to indicate a
state of unorganized potentiality (cf. "To the Madon-
na"), here it appears as a locus of blindness, dread, and
error: striving to become as god, man is instead reduced
to animality. A few mortals, however, have retained a
glimmer of the divine fire within their breasts; through
such men, the gods may become manifest (for the de-
pendency of the gods upon mortals, see strophe 8 of
"The Rhine").

PAGE 159   The "prophetic ones" who shine high in the sky like yel-
low starfire also come to the aid of the Father, allowing

the divine to be revealed in "torn times." It is to these
celestial figures (and to the eagle, herald of the gods)
that poets must look, lest they lose themselves in merely
solipsistic interpretations of God's will. Hellingrath calls
these lines "one of the most powerful and beautiful sen-
tences ever built in German."

Hercules and the Dioscuri are among the "prophetic
ones" alluded to in the previous passage. The demigod
Hercules is a (Christ-like) savior who cleanses the earth
of monstrosity and descends into the underworld to re-
deem the dead. Philoctetes kindles the pyre upon which
Hercules is finally consumed by divine fire and for this
act of mercy is rewarded with the demigod's bow. The
regular rise and fall of the Dioscuri in the heavens sug-
gests an achieved measure between high and low, earth
and sky. The constellation of the Twins, sacred to navi-
gators, is an emblem of that celestial harmony associ-
ated with the teachings of Pythagoras.

PAGE 161   The poem returns to the "untimely growth" and blind,
senseless activity of mortals previously evoked in lines
28-56 (pp. 155-157). Cf. Shelley's *Prometheus Bound*,
act 1, ll. 165ff.

[There was a time . . .] / [Sonst nemlich, Vater Zevs . . .]

PAGE 163   *Diana.* According to some legends, the goddess Diana
participated in the battle against the Titans.

the angry/Lord. The notion of anger or wrath (*Zorn*)
recurs frequently in Hölderlin's late work, often
associated with the figure of the Father (see Jean
Laplanche's psychoanalytic study *Hölderlin et la question
du père*). In this poem, as elsewhere, the wrathful
presence of the demiurgic Father is at once revealed and
concealed in thunderclouds and discharged as
apocalyptic lightning. In the gathering storm the poet
asks that his native land be spared from the fiery
immediacy of the Lord and offers to sacrifice his own
life to the Fury (Erinys) instead.

[Do you think . . .] / [Meinest du es solle gehen . . .]

As Hölderlin explains in his letter to Böhlendorff of December 4,
1801, the Greeks achieved such mastery in art and in clarity of repre-

sentation that in the end they forgot those qualities that were truly innate or national to them, that is, passionate "aorgic" excess, Apollonian fire. The reverse is true of the Hesperidean Germans. See Introduction, pp. 13-14.

The Eagle / Der Adler

I follow the text given by Sattler in the *Einleitung* to the *Frankfurter Ausgabe.*

Herald of the coming gods, the eagle here follows the course of the Westering of the Spirit: from India, to Greece, to Italy, and then northward toward the St. Gotthard pass, source of the rivers Rhine, Ticino, Rhône, Aare, and Reuss.

PAGE 167   *Etruria.* Roughly coincides with the region of present-day Tuscany.

                Haimos. Mountain range in northern Thrace.

                Athos. Mountain in northeastern Greece, known for its monastery.

                Lemnos. The marooned Philoctetes spent ten years living in the caves of the island of Lemnos before being rescued by Neoptolemos and Odysseus.

[Alps . . .] / [Ihr sichergebaueten Alpen . . .]

A song of praise to the poet's native Swabia. The Weinsteig ("vineyard path") is a road on the outskirts of Stuttgart with a fine view of the city. The Spitzberg is a mountain near Tübingen: an ancient Roman road runs along its western flank. Johann Jakob Thill (1747–1772) was a minor local poet whom Hölderlin admired.

The Nearest the Best / Das Nächste Beste

Fall 1803? Three different versions of this poem exist. I have followed the text constituted by Sattler for his *Frankfurter Ausgabe.*

For the first six lines of the poem see the notes to "The Titans." The "windows of heaven" may be taken from the account of the Flood in Genesis 7:11, ". . . the fountains of the great deep [were] broken up, and the windows of heaven were opened."

The title of the hymn (literally, "that which is nearest is best") is picked up in line 35 (p. 177): starlings, quickened by the breeze that blows from Germany, fly back home from southern France, drawn to what is nearest or most native to them. The course of migratory birds thus embodies what Hölderlin elsewhere terms *vaterländische Umkehr,* reversion to the Fatherland. Having experienced the intoxication of divine fire in foreign parts (Greece, southern France), the spirit swerves back to the more lucid climes of home; only through venturing into radical otherness can one learn to grasp those elusive immediacies that lie closest at hand. As Heidegger observes in his "Brief über den Humanismus": "Being is that which is nearest. But nearnesss remains the furthest thing from man."

Although contemporary historical events (particularly the Napoleonic Wars) indicate that the time is not yet ripe for the gods to return to Germany (ll. 43ff. [p. 177]), the landscape of southern Germany evoked toward the close of the poem lies poised in anticipation.

The two concluding sections of the hymn are cryptic. Sattler suggests that the shelter (*Winkel*) refers to the tilted stones at Hahrdt (see p. 256). "The spirit was/The horse's flesh" alludes to Isaiah 31:3, "Now the Egyptians are men, and not God; and their horses flesh, and not spirit." The following lines, Sattler observes, refer to the three manners in which the Spirit may manifest itself: in prophecy (the ominous eagles over Ilion), in song, and in judgment.

Tinian

Tinian is a South Pacific island described in the widely read account of Admiral George Anson's *Voyage Round the World in the Years 1740–44* (1748). By the late eighteenth century the name Tinian had become synonymous with the state of nature in its most exotic and utopian guise (see Rousseau's *La Nouvelle Héloïse*, pt. 4, letter 11). The poem's title would therefore seem to imply that paradise is not to be found on some South Sea isle of the blest but rather here, in the present, on native ground.

Columbus / Kolomb

This fragmentary Columbiad, first drafted in 1801 and further elaborated in 1805 to 1806, may have been intended as part of a cycle dealing with the various heroes of the modern (or Hesperidean) age. In a letter to Seckendorf of March 12, 1804, Hölderlin notes that he is currently very much occupied with "fable" (or myth), that is, with "the poetic aspect of history and the architectonics of heaven . . . and especially with national [myth] inasmuch as it differs from the Greek." The letter continues: "I have outlined the various destinies of heroes, knights, and princes, how they serve fate or act more or less ambiguously in relation to it."

Sattler suggests that this poem was in part inspired by Hölderlin's reading of Herder, in particular that section of *Adrastea* in which Herder proposes Columbus as a promising topic for epic. "A New World, both moral and physical, lies before the poet's eyes, which he could present in opposition to the ancient hemisphere. For many centuries the guardian spirit of that younger continent protected it from the sight of its elder sister, but fate will have its way; the age of discovery nears, sped by the greed of nations, implacable. In vain does the guardian spirit of those infant lands beyond the sea try everything in its power to ward off the discovery, delaying the event until the culture and politics of Europe . . . will have become purer and more humane. But the thirst for discovery, excited by the Crusades, by science, by poverty and depravity, has been inflamed; it culminates in Columbus."

As in "Patmos" the voice and memory of the poet gradually modulate into those of the poem's protagonist. The central section of the poem (roughly from line 35 [p. 187] through the phrase "You are all this in your beauty apocalyptica" [p. 189] is presumably spoken by Columbus himself, and appears to narrate the preparations for the expedition, the blessing of the ships, the squabbles among the crew, their greed for gain, etc. The French phrases that punctuate the text in Poundian fashion may be snippets overheard in the port of Bordeaux; the French, at any rate, is pure Hölderlinian idiolect. I have followed the new, considerably expanded reading of this text included in Sattler's *Frankfurter Ausgabe*

PAGE 185   *Anson.* Lord George Anson (1697–1762), English explorer of the early eighteenth century; see the note to "Tinian."

            Gama. Vasco da Gama (1450–1524), Portuguese discoverer of the sea passage to India.

            Aeneas. Presumably included in the catalogue not only as a navigator but as founder of the new eon of Rome.

            Jason. Leader of the expedition of the Argonauts, raised as a child by the centaur Chiron.

            Megara. Vergil was felled by a sunstroke at Megara while visiting Greece; his condition grew worse on the sea voyage home and soon after landing, he died at Brundisium.

            Templars. The Crusaders.

            Bouillon, Rinaldo. Crusaders in Tasso's *Gerusalemme Liberata*.

            Bougainville. Louis Antoine de Bougainville (1729–1811), French explorer and author of a *Voyage autour du monde* (1771).

PAGE 187   *ils crient rapport . . . un saisrien.* They scream: profit (or report); he [replies]: close your house; you are a know-nothing.

PAGE 189   *entiere personne . . . rapport tire.* Self-satisfied in his entire person; difficult knowledge; make a sworn report (or reap profit?).

PAGE 191   *moments tirees . . . hautes sommeils.* Moments drawn from elevated dreams.
lui a les pleures. He has tears.

[And to experience . . .] / [Und mitzufühlen das Leben . . .]

The remaining poems in these selections of *Drafts of Hymns* are generally believed to date from 1805 to 1806: they a therefore among the last texts Hölderlin wrote before he was committed to the Autenrieth Clinic. Despite the patient paleographic labors of Hellingrath, Beissner, and, more recently, Sattler, a number of the readings remain conjectural.

[The fruits are ripe . . .] / [Reif sind . . .]

This text was originally published by Hellingrath as an independent lyric poem to be grouped with *Nightsongs* (see p. 255). Following Beissner's persuasive example, subsequent editors have situated these lines as the first strophe of the third version of "Mnemosyne" (see p. 268). Sattler, however, has recently disputed this reading: in his *Frankfurter Ausgabe* this text instead constitutes the first portion of a large mosaic of late fragments he has gathered under the collective title "Apriorität des Individuellen."

[We set out from the abyss . . .] / [Vom Abgrund nemlich . . .]

In the *Frankfurter Ausgabe* a somewhat different reading of this text appears as the third and final portion of "Apriorität des Individuellen." While following Sattler's order, I have preferred Beissner's version of the poem.

[The Vatican . . .] / [Der Vatikan . . .]

Hellingrath was the first to point out that many of the images in this poem derive from Wilhelm Heinse, Hölderlin's "respected master/Over in Westphalia" (ll. 10-11). Heinse's utopian romance *Ardinghello or the Isles of the Blest* (1787) not only proposed an idealization of Greece that was to have a profound impact on Hölderlin's *Hyperion* but also evoked Rome and the Vatican at the time of the Renaissance.

PAGE 203   *the spirit of Julius.* Julius Caesar reformed the calendar in
46 B.C.

the young man in the desert. John the Baptist. Cf. Matthew
3:4.

Loreto. Heinse mentions Tasso's pilgrimage to Loreto in
his introduction to his translation of *Gerusalemme Libe-
rata* (1781).

PAGE 205   *Turkish.* Alludes to the Ottoman rule over Greece (Morea
is the medieval name for the Peloponnesos).

the owl, familiar from scripture. Cf. Isaiah 13:21, " . . . and
their houses shall be full of doleful creatures; and owls
shall dwell there, and satyrs shall dance there." Or
Psalm 102:6, "I am like a pelican of the wilderness: I
am like an owl of the desert."

The bridesong of heaven. See strophe 13 of "The Rhine."

a work/Of total proportion. In his essay "Hölderlin's Erde
und Himmel" (included in his *Erläuterungen*), Heideg-
ger relates these lines to the fourfold of Earth-Sky-God-
Man, the "infinite relation" known as Fate (*Geschick*).

Greece / Griechenland

I follow Sattler's recent reconstruction of this text, which convinc-
ingly splices together what had previously been considered three sepa-
rate versions of the poem. Heidegger comments at length on "Greece"
in his essay "Hölderlins Erde und Himmel."

PAGE 207   *In the school's open air.* The German reads *an der Schule
Blau.* This "blue" suggested an open air school, perhaps
the Lyceum near the temple of Apollo Lukeios where
Aristotle taught.

PAGE 211   *a rustle / Of laurels.* The site of Vergil's grave in the vol-
canic landscape of Naples was described in detail in
Heinse's *Ardinghello.*

Windsor. May allude to the marriage of Prince Friedrich of
Württemberg and the British Princess Charlotte in
1797. The ceremony took place in London and was
subsequently celebrated at Windsor Castle.

[What is the life of man . . .] / *[Was ist der Menschen Leben . . .]*

[What is God . . .] / *[Was ist Gott . . .]*

Though Beissner dates these two texts around 1802, I follow the Hellingrath Edition in placing them here, given their close thematic affinities to "Greece." Both texts also offer a bridge into "In lovely blue" (see p. 249).

Fragments

I have made a selection from the ninety-one miscellaneous texts that are collected in most Hölderlin editions under the title *Pläne und Bruchstücke* ("Drafts and Fragments"). It is virtually impossible to date any of these texts with certainty, but most of the poems I have translated here seem to be quite late, between 1803 and 1806.

Untitled fragment

Apparently the draft of a "native song" dealing with the exploits of the great German heroes of the past (see notes to "Columbus").

PAGE 231 *Friedrich with his bitten cheek.* Friedrich Landgrave of Thüringen (1237–1324), who, after the death of Conradin in 1268, was encouraged by the Lombard Ghibellines to enter into opposition against Charles of Anjou.
Barbarossa. Frederick I of Germany (1123?–1190), the greatest of all the Hohenstaufer and hence the most significant of Swabian heroes to Hölderlin.
Conradin. The last of the great Swabian Hohenstaufer; he died in Naples at age sixteen in 1268.
Ugolino. The thirteenth-century Ghibelline Count whom Dante portrays in Canto 33 of the *Inferno*.
Eugenius. Prince of Savoy (1663–1736).

Untitled fragment

PAGE 233 *Mohammed, Rinaldo* [a character in Tasso's *Gerusalemme*], and *Barbarossa.* All evoke the Crusades.
Heinrich. Emperor Heinrich IV of Germany, who crossed the Alps on his way to Canossa (see notes to the later version of "Patmos"). His eldest son, *Conrad,* died in 1101.
Demetrius Poliorcetes (337–283 B.C.). One of the Diadochoi of Alexander the Great; named King of Macedonia.
Peter the Great (1672–1725). Czar of Russia.

Untitled fragment

A visionary gazeteer composed on the back of a laundry bill. Its various toponymic resonances indicate, as Hölderlin notes in an 1802 letter to Böhlendorff, "the way in which the diversities of nature all converge in one area, so that all the holy places of the earth come together in a single place." An eloquent example of the poetics of pure naming, this onamastic catalogue forms an intricate ideogram in which elements of Hölderlinian landscape (mountains, rivers, valleys, islands, liminal sites) are interfused with the destinies of exceptional men and women. Beissner (*Hölderlin-Jahrbuch*, 1947) provides a useful gloss.

PAGE 235   *Tende.* Former earldom in the Piedmont; now a French town in the Alpes Maritimes on the Italian border.

Strömfeld. Johann Carl von Strömfeld, general in the army of the Swedish King Charles XII?

Simonetta. Could refer to one of the members of the Simonetta family, prominent in the life and letters of fifteenth- and sixteenth-century Italy.

Teufen. Swiss town in the canton of Appenzell, possibly associated with Hölderlin's sojourn in Hauptwil (1801).

Amyclae. Ancient Greek town near Sparta, famed for its cult of Apollo. Seat of King Tyndareos, father of Helen, Clytaemnestra, and the Dioscuri.

Aveiro. Portuguese city. Situated by the sea near the mouth of the river Vouga, its geography rhymes with that of Bordeaux.

Alencastro. According to Hölderlin's source (*Zedlers Lexicon*), the family d'Alencastro took its title of nobility from the city of Aveiro.

Amalasuntha. Queen of the Ostrogoths (498–535). Her wide learning and commitment to the cultural values of Rome earned her the enmity of rival Goth factions. Banished to the Tuscan lake of Bolsena, she was murdered in her bath.

Antegon. Alternate reading: Antagon. Antigone?

Ardinghellus. A reference to Heinse's utopian romance *Ardinghello und die glückseligen Inseln* (1787)?

Celestine. Pope Celestine V (1215–1290)?

Innocent. Pope Innocent IV (?–1254)?

Aloisia Sigea. Louise Sigea de Velasco (1530–1560). Celebrated in Spain and Portugal for her vast erudition; author of the *Dialogus de differentia vitae rusticae et urbanae* cited in this and the following line.

Thermodon. River flowing from the mountains of Cappadocia in Asia Minor into the Black Sea. Mentioned in Ovid's *Metamorphoses* and Aeschylus's *Prometheus.*

Valtelino. I.e., Valtellina, mountainous region in northern Lombardy bordering on Switzerland.

Schönberg. Common German place name. May refer to the town in the Bayrischer Wald on the edge of Bohemia.

Scotus. Either the philosopher Erigena (?–875?) or the theologian Duns Scotus (1265?–1308).

Tenerife. One of the Canary Islands.

Sulaco. Mountain range and river in Honduras. Or possibly a deformation of Soulac, a town at the tip of the Médoc Peninsula near Bordeaux.

Venafro. Town in the Italian province of Campobasso. Founded, according to legend, by Diomedes and known for its earthquakes.

Zamora. Capital of the Spanish province of the same name. Also a place name in Mexico and Ecuador.

Jacca. I.e., Jaca, Spanish town at the foot of the Pyrenees in the province of Huesca.

Genoa. See the poem'"Columbus."

Larissa. Capital of Thessaly.

In Lovely Blue

This text is drawn from Wilhelm Waiblinger's novel *Phaeton* (1823). Waiblinger was a young college student in Tübingen and an ardent admirer of Hölderlin who frequently visited the poet in his tower during the years 1822 to 1826. The hero of Waiblinger's novel, the mad sculptor Phaeton, is modeled after Hölderlin, and this text is offered (in prose form) by the narrator as a specimen of the artist's insanity: "He would cover all the paper he could lay his hands on with writing. Here are a few pages taken from his papers which give a good idea of his terribly distraught state of mind. In the original they are divided into lines of verse, in Pindaric fashion." This comment encouraged Ludwig von Pigenot to recast the prose text into its "original" verse form: I have followed his reconstruction, printed in volume 6 of the Hellingrath edition. Beissner and other editors print this text in prose (if at all), while disputing its authenticity. André du Bouchet, who translated the poem for the Pléiade edition of Hölderlin, comments: "The unsurpassed beauty and, what's more, the coherence of this poem, render such conjectures futile." "In lovely blue . . ." is a central text in Heidegger's canon; see especially his essays "Hölderlin and the Essence of Poetry" and " . . . Poetically Man Dwells. . . . "

A Brief Bibliography of Hölderlin in English

Translations

Burford, William, and Middleton, Christopher, eds. *The Poet's Vocation.* Austin, 1968. (Includes letters by Hölderlin.)
Gascoyne, David. *Hölderlin's Madness.* London, 1938.
Hamburger, Michael. *Selected Verse.* Harmondsworth, 1961.
———. *Poems and Fragments.* Rev. ed. Cambridge, 1980.
Henderson, Elizabeth. *Alcaic Poems.* New York, 1963.
Leishman, J. B. *Selected Poems.* London, 1938.
Middleton, Christopher. *Selected Poems.* Chicago, 1972.
Prokosch, Frederick. *Some Poems of Friedrich Hölderlin.* Norfolk, 1943.
Trask, Willard. *Hyperion.* New York, 1965.

Monographs

Benn, M. B. *Hölderlin and Pindar.* 'S-Gravenhage, 1962.
Constantine, David. *The Significance of Locality in the Poetry of Friedrich Hölderlin.* London, 1979.
Fehervary, Helen. *Hölderlin and the Left.* Heidelberg, 1977.
George, Emery. *Hölderlin's "Ars Poetica": A Part-Rigorous Analysis of Information Structure in the Late Hymns.* 'S-Gravenhage, 1973.
———, ed. *Friederich Hölderlin: An Early Modern.* Ann Arbor, 1972.
Harrison, R. B. *Hölderlin and Greek Literature.* Oxford, 1975.
Montgomery, Marshall. *Friedrich Hölderlin and the German Neo-Hellenic Movement.* Oxford, 1923.
Peacock, Ronald. *Hölderlin.* London, 1938.
Quarterly Review of Literature 10, nos. 1–2. 1959.
Salzberger, L. S. *Hölderlin.* New Haven, 1952.
Shelton, Roy C. *The Young Hölderlin.* Bern, 1973.
Silz, Walter. *Hölderlin's Hyperion: A Critical Reading.* Philadelphia, 1969.
Stahl, E. L. *Hölderlin's Symbolism.* Oxford, 1945.
Stansfield, Agnes. *Hölderlin.* Manchester, 1943.
Unger, Richard. *Hölderlin's Major Poetry.* Bloomington, 1975.

Index of German Titles

Index of English Titles

The Lockert Library of Poetry in Translation

George Seferis: Collected Poems (1924–1955), translated, edited, and introduced by Edmund Keeley and Philip Sherrard

Collected Poems of Lucio Piccolo, translated and edited by Brian Swann and Ruth Feldman

C. P. Cavafy: Collected Poems, translated by Edmund Keeley and Philip Sherrard and edited by George Savidis

Benny Andersen: Selected Poems, translated by Alexander Taylor

Selected Poetry of Andrea Zanzotto, translated and edited by Ruth Feldman and Brian Swann

Poems of René Char, translated by Mary Ann Caws and Jonathan Griffin

Selected Poems of Tudor Arghezi, translated and edited by Michael Impey and Brian Swann

"The Survivor" and Other Poems by Tadeusz Różewicz, translated and introduced by Magnus J. Krynski and Robert A. Maguire

"Harsh World" and Other Poems by Ángel González, translated by Donald D. Walsh

Ritsos in Parentheses, translations and introduction by Edmund Keeley

Salamander: Selected Poems of Robert Marteau, translated by Anne Winters

Angelos Sikelianos: Selected Poems, translated and introduced by Edmund Keeley and Philip Sherrard

Dante's "Rime," translated by Patrick S. Diehl

Selected Later Poems of Marie Luise Kaschnitz, translated by Lisel Mueller

Osip Mandelstam's "Stone," translated and introduced by Robert Tracy

The Dawn Is Always New: Selected Poetry of Rocco Scotellaro, translated by Ruth Feldman and Brian Swann

Sounds, Feelings, Thoughts: Seventy Poems by Wisława Szymborska, translated and introduced by Magnus J. Krynski and Robert A. Maguire

The Man I Pretend to Be: "The Colloquies" and Selected Poems of Guido Gozzano, translated and edited by Michael Palma, with an introductory essay by Eugenio Montale

D'Après Tout: Poems by Jean Follain, translated by Heather McHugh

Songs of Something Else: Selected Poems of Gunnar Ekelöf, translated by Leonard Nathan and James Larson

The Little Treasury of One Hundred People, One Poem Each, compiled
  by Fujiwara No Sadaie and translated by Tom Galt
The Ellipse: Selected Poems of Leonardo Sinisgalli, translated by W. S. Di
  Piero
The Difficult Days by Roberto Sosa, translated by Jim Lindsey
Hymns and Fragments by Friedrich Hölderlin, translated and
  introduced by Richard Sieburth
The Silence Afterwards: Selected Poems of Rolf Jacobsen, translated and
  edited by Roger Greenwald
Rilke: Between Roots, selected poems rendered from the German
  by Rika Lesser
In the Storm of the Roses: Selected Poems by Ingborg Bachmann, translated,
  edited, and introduced by Mark Anderson
Birds and Other Relations: Selected Poetry of Dezsó Tandori, translated
  by Bruce Berlind
Brocade River Poems: Selected Works of the Tang Dynasty Couresan Xue Tao,
  translated and introduced by Jeanne Larsen
The True Subject: Selected Poems of Faiz Ahmed Faiz, translated
  by Naomi Lazard
My Name on the Wind: Selected Poems of Diego Valeri, translated
  by Michael Palma
Aeschylus: The Suppliants, translated by
  Peter Burian
Foamy Sky: The Major Poems of Miklós Radnóti, selected and translated
  by Zsuzsanna Ozváth and Frederick Turner
La Fontaine's Bawdy: Of Libertines, Louts and Lechers, translated
  by Norman R. Shapiro
A Child Is Not a Knife: Selected Poems of Göran Sonnevi, translated and
  edited by Rika Lesser
George Seferis: Collected Poems, Revised Edition, translated, edited and
  introduced by Edmund Keeley and Phillip Sherrard
Selected Poems of Shmuel HaNagid, translated from the Hebrew
  by Peter Cole
The Late Poems of Meng Chiao, translated by David Hinton